Sight Cast

Leading with Impact & Fulfillment

A FIELD GUIDE FOR LEADERS

John Haydock

Published by Sight Casting LLC

Copyright © 2026 John Haydock
All rights reserved.

Published by Sight Casting LLC

Charlottesville, Virginia

No part of this book may be reproduced, stored in a retrieval system, or transmitted in any form or by any means—electronic, mechanical, photocopying, recording, or otherwise—without the prior written permission of the publisher, except in the case of brief quotations embodied in critical articles and reviews.

This book is a work of nonfiction. In some instances, names and identifying details have been changed to protect privacy. Any examples are presented for illustrative purposes and are not intended to depict any specific person or organization unless explicitly stated.

First edition

ISBN: 979-8-9942356-0-7 (Paperback)

Cover design: John Haydock

Interior art: "Bonefishing Belize" & "John Casting Alaska" © 2026 Rebecca Haydock. Used with permission.

Photography: Drake Haydock, Cove Haydock, and John Haydock

Printed in the United States of America

Disclaimer

The information in this book is for educational and informational purposes only and is not intended as medical, psychological, or professional advice. The use of Acceptance and Commitment Therapy (ACT) principles in this book is focused on leadership development and should not replace consultation with a qualified healthcare professional. All trademarks are the property of their respective owners. Any use of trademarks is for identification purposes only and does not imply endorsement.

To my wife, Rebecca, and our sons, Drake and Cove—any notion of impact or fulfillment begins at home with you.

Table of Contents

INTRODUCTION 1
PART I: CURIOSITY 10
    Chapter 1 – A Short History of the Science of Happiness 11
    Chapter 2 – What The Research Tells Us 18
    Chapter 3 – Seeing Yourself Clearly 28
    Chapter 4 – Life Stages, Transitions, and the Shocks of Life 37
PART II: AIM 48
    Chapter 5 – What are you Really Aiming At? 49
    Chapter 6 – Impact: The Difference You Are Making 58
    Chapter 7 – Identity 69
PART III: SEND IT 82
    Chapter 8 – Send It: Making the First Cast Count 83
    Chapter 9 – Working With the River: ACT for Hard Casts .. 89
    Chapter 10 – Leading with Recommendations 97
    Chapter 11 – Invest in High-Trust Relationships 107
    Chapter 12 – How Feedback Fuels Trust and Impact 113
    Chapter 13 – Shaping Your Work 125
    Chapter 14 – Peak Experiences and Flow 131
PART IV: TEND IT & TRACK 139
    Chapter 15 – Tracking and Recalibration 140
    Chapter 16 – Your Personal Strategy Compass 151
CONCLUSION: FORWARD C.A.S.T. 163
TOOLKIT 168
    Values and Impact Exercise 170
    Calendar & Commitments Audit 172

SAYING "NO" as Stewardship Filters 173
"Designing Freshness" Exercise 174
Check In – Acceptance and Commitment Therapy (ACT) . 177
In The Moment: Field Checklist 180
Personal Compass – Curiosity, Aim, Send It, and Tend It .. 181
ADDITIONAL EXPLORATORY 188
REFERENCES 190
ACKNOWLEDGEMENTS 197
ABOUT THE AUTHOR 200

INTRODUCTION

"It is not that we have a short time to live, but that we waste so much of it."

—Seneca

Why This Book, and Why Now

You are a leader who carries a lot—responsible for business outcomes, boards, aging parents, children, and community. Your resume is impressive. People rely on you. You deliver results.

And yet, there may be a quieter set of questions: If I keep living this way for 10 or 20 more years, what will that do to my health, my relationships, my sense of self? Am I moving toward a life that feels meaningful and exciting, or am I simply making it through obligations? How do I hold myself and others to a high standard without burning out or becoming resentful? **Am I happy?**

Those questions are not indulgent. For leaders with a heavy load of responsibility, they are strategic. Your happiness and fulfillment are not separate from your effectiveness; they are upstream of your ability to think clearly, make good decisions, hold people accountable, and stay the course when things are hard.

This book grew out of that reality—and my own experience. It is a field guide, co-created by you, for changing how you live and lead in the moments that matter. It will help you make different decisions about what you say yes and no to, design a calendar that reflects your priorities, enter hard conversations with clearer intent, and update your sense of who you are as your roles and seasons change. It is written for leaders who are quietly exhausted, whose success feels misdirected, and who are stuck in heroic but unsustainable patterns of over-functioning. Instead of offering generic inspiration or one more list of leadership hacks, Sight Cast uses the C.A.S.T. framework—Curiosity, Aim, Send It, Tend It & Track—grounded in the realities of life stages, Acceptance and Commitment Therapy, and a simple river-and-casting metaphor.

This isn't a book about fishing. When I talk about casts, currents, or reading the water, I'm using them as metaphors for the choices you're already making. If you've never picked up a fly rod, the principles work just the same. You'll see how to build a culture of accountability where people bring recommendations, not just problems, and you'll have concrete tools—like the field checklist in the appendix—to use when you're tired, under pressure, and tempted to fall back into old habits.

Most leaders I work with aren't unfulfilled because they're failing. On paper, they're doing well—but they feel restless and a bit like imposters, sensing something is missing. Usually, it's because their success is misdirected in one or more of these ways:

1. **Over-cast for achievement**, chasing goals and wins without asking whether they deliver meaningful impact.

2. **Under-aim their own lives**, being deliberate about the organization while being vague about their own direction.

3. **Reinforce cultures that escalate problems,** leading teams that bring you issues instead of recommendations.

4. **Drift without a personal compass**, tracking the business relentlessly while never tending to what matters most.

The C.A.S.T. framework is the operating system for that recalibration. It is a tight loop you can run in your head when you're tired, under pressure, and overscheduled. It is a tool to use in moments that matter most:

Curiosity - Get curious about your tendencies, history, and values. Look at other people's pressures and constraints, and what science tells us about fulfillment and effectiveness. Curiosity widens the lens.

Aim - Decide what you're aiming for. Given what you've seen, what do you want in this season? Which "fish" are worth going after? Aim is where values and best practices turn into concrete choices about where you will and won't spend energy.

Send It - Act. Have a hard conversation, give the feedback, set the boundary, take the next step. Many leaders stay in their heads. Send It is about moving from rumination to action and building cultures where people bring recommended solutions, not just problems.

Tend It & Track - After you act, tend the relationships and track what happens. When the "fish" don't rise, change flies and adjust your approach. Tend It & Track is where you notice the response and keep learning, instead of drifting.

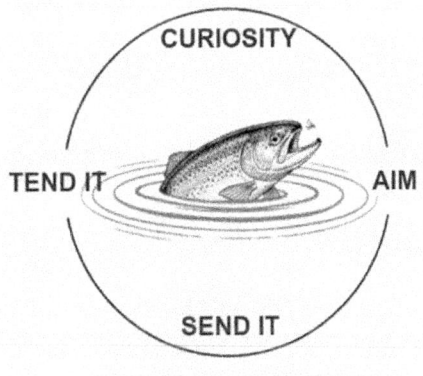

The C.A.S.T. Framework

I spent decades chasing achievement—titles, recognition, income, conventional markers of success. Some was necessary. Some was ego. Some was fear that if I stopped achieving, I'd stop mattering.

Gradually, something shifted—through hard conversations, mistakes, losses, and the slow accumulation of evidence that the life I was building didn't match the life I wanted. I began to choose differently. **I left bigger roles for mission-aligned work.** I walked away from income and status to work in brands and causes I believed in. I said no to opportunities that would look good on a résumé but felt wrong in my gut. I built flexibility into my work so I could show up for my kids and, later, for my aging parents. I didn't do this out of obligation, but because I wanted to. I devoted more time to community and causes I felt strongly about. I accepted board leadership roles at American Rivers, where the work has impact but there's no paycheck—just purpose.

Those choices came with real tradeoffs: financial cost, professional visibility, and the quiet question—Did I just give up something I can't get back?

Here's what I've learned: **the tradeoffs were worth it.** Not because the path got easier but because the effort started to feel like mine. The discomfort became the price of admission for a life that aligns with who I am and what I value. I've also learned that this work is never done. My parents' needs increase. My kids' lives change. My capacity shifts. The river moves. I adjust.

I have watched peers and clients—senior leaders, founders, and professionals with enormous capacity—wrestle with the same tensions: caring deeply about their work and the people they lead while feeling pulled apart by competing demands. Many are quietly managing health issues, family complexity, past losses, or private fears that their life is out of balance. Some carry a long-standing pattern of over-functioning—always scanning for what could go wrong, always stepping in—shaped by early experiences that taught them to be hyper-vigilant and self-reliant.

If you're a leader carrying a heavy load you already know what I'm talking about. You know the weight and the tradeoffs. You know the temptation to keep grinding and hope it works out.

But here's the thing: if you don't tend to your own well-being, you erode your capacity to lead well. If you don't stay connected to values, you drift toward expediency. If you don't build a pace you can maintain, you burn out or disappear inside obligations. When we as leaders ignore that, systems and people pay a price.

This book does not come from abstract theory. Over the past decade, I've worked as an executive coach and advisor to CEOs, founders, board members, and operators navigating the complexity of high-stakes roles and full lives. Before that, I spent thirty years as a leader: running businesses from startups to billion-dollar portfolios, building teams, serving on corporate and nonprofit boards, and making the kinds of tradeoffs this book explores. This work draws on that experience, the science of well-being and leadership, and hundreds of conversations with leaders trying to do the same thing you are—lead with impact without losing themselves in the process.

Sight Casting is the metaphor I'm using in this book, but it is not the origin. The origin is that tension you may recognize in yourself: being deeply responsible for others and for outcomes, while also wanting to **live a life that "lights me up," feels secure, and lets me be at peace.**

Sight Casting as a Metaphor

I am not here to hand you a magic formula. I'm here as a guide, the way a fishing guide stands beside you on the river. A good guide doesn't fish for you. They help you read the water. They point out currents, obstacles, and opportunities you might miss on your own. They provide some tools—the rod, reel, and flies—and show you how to use them. They suggest where to stand, how to cast, and offer new approaches when helpful.

But you still do the work. You feel the line in your hands and decide where and when to cast. You live with the consequences of your choices. You'll see stories from days on the river throughout these pages, because fly fishing has been one of the clearest teachers in my life.

I know fly fishing can carry a reputation—expensive lodges, exotic destinations, and a sport for executives with money to burn. That's not how I came to it, and it's not what I'm asking you to do. I started fly fishing when I was in the 6th grade after our family moved from upstate New York to rural North Carolina. I felt alone in a new neighborhood and school. I retreated to books, magazines, and time outside. I bought my first fly rod for about $15 at the local hardware store and taught myself to cast in the pond behind our house. Over time, fly fishing faded in and out of my life during different life stages, and what it meant to me changed—adventure, learning, accomplishment, intimate time with friends, time in nature, self-discovery.

Most of us spend large stretches of our lives blind casting: throwing energy, time, and ambition in every direction we can, hoping to land something—success, security, recognition, maybe happiness. We are constantly busy, often externally successful, but not always intentional about what we are aiming at or honest about what it is costing us.

Sight Casting is about **being curious and seeing clearly**—your reality, your values, the conditions under which you flourish. It's about **choosing deliberately,** aiming not just at achievement, but at a blend of impact and happiness. It is **acting with intention**—casting fewer, more deliberate lines instead of living in constant overextension. It requires **learning and adjusting**—treating life as a series of experiments, not a fixed script.

In fly fishing, sight casting means making deliberate casts after spotting your target, not just casting blindly. Sight casting isn't a separate kind of fishing. It means you see your target—like a specific fish or a shadow, or a swirl—and you cast on purpose to that spot. You can do that with spin gear, baitcasting gear, or a fly rod; what matters is the intentional, aimed cast. Applying that precision to leadership and life, Sight Cast is a field guide for leaders seeking impact and fulfillment, grounded in a commitment to honor your responsibility to others and to yourself.

Who This Book Is For

This book is for senior leaders in the "sandwich years"—executives, founders, and operators balancing peak professional influence with peak personal obligations. You may be raising or launching children, supporting aging parents, navigating your own health, and carrying board or community responsibilities. It is for you if you care deeply about meaningful impact but notice strain: fatigue, cynicism, or the quiet feeling that your days have become obligations to manage rather than a life to live. If you suspect the next milestone won't create the fulfillment you want, and you're willing to run a new loop, this is for you. This is not a book for those looking for an escape hatch. It will not tell you to quit your job and move to a cabin in the woods. Most leaders I work with don't want to escape; they want more clarity, presence, and peace.

This book assumes a few things. You will likely **stay in the arena**—continuing to lead and show up for the people who depend on you. You want to do that in a sustainable and fulfilling way. And you will remain curious about research, frameworks, and stories from other leaders. This book invites you to sight cast your life: to look clearly at your reality, to aim at what matters, to take small steps, and to track what you learn.

Along the way, I will draw on –

The science of happiness and fulfillment—what research tells us (and doesn't tell us) about what makes life feel worth living.

Acceptance and Commitment Therapy (ACT) and related approaches that help you act in line with your values, even in the presence of discomfort. (Hayes et al., 2011; Harris, 2009)

Peak and optimal experience research—what we know about those moments of deep engagement and meaning, and how to invite more of them without chasing highs.

Personality frameworks (like the Enneagram, MBTI, Hogan, and DiSC) as maps—not verdicts—to understand your patterns of striving and stress.

Philosophical lenses such as Stoicism and contemporary work on emotional agility, to help you reconcile acceptance and agency. (David, 2016)

Life stages and shocks—young kids, career transitions, losses, unexpected joys—that reshape our values and path to happiness.

Throughout, I return to a simple premise: happiness and fulfillment aren't the opposite of impact; they're the soil in which durable leadership grows. My role is to help you read the water of your own life more clearly and choose casts more intentionally.

You'll still do the work. This book simply aims to make that work more grounded in research and aligned with the happiness, fulfillment, and impact you want.

Three Terms That Will Guide This Work

Throughout this book, three concepts recur as touchstones: **Values**, **Identity**, and **Impact**.

Values are your chosen life directions—the qualities of action that matter deeply to you. In Acceptance and Commitment Therapy (ACT), values aren't goals you complete; they're ongoing directions (Hayes et al., 2011). They answer the question: "What kind of person do I want to be in my actions?"

Identity is your sense of who you are: operator, advisor, parent, caregiver, mentor. It's both social and internal, shifting across life stages often faster than we realize.

Impact is the difference your actions make—on people, organizations, and communities. It's about consequences, not just intentions. It answers: "What changes because I showed up?"

Leaders run into trouble when these three drift out of alignment. Roles change faster than identity. Stated values drift from how you spend time. Or you chase achievement long after it stops moving the needle on well-being or impact. This work is about clarifying values, updating identity to fit your current season, and designing your calendar so you can say: **"Imperfect as it is, this is the impact I want to have—and a life I actually want to live."**

In the chapters ahead, we start with curiosity. Decades of research offer clarity on the foundations of happiness and fulfillment—patterns that show up across people, careers, and life stages.

PART I: CURIOSITY

Seeing You and Your Situation Clearly

Before you can cast toward your target, you have to get curious about the water you're standing in. You need to explore the currents, notice where the fish might be feeding, and recognize your own position on the riverbank.

Part I is about cultivating that kind of **curiosity**—about the science of happiness and fulfillment, about your own patterns and blind spots, and about the context of your life stage and circumstances.

This curiosity isn't optional. Without it, you're casting blind, hoping for the best. With it, you can aim with more honesty and adjust with more wisdom as the river changes.

C.A.S.T.
Curiosity - Aim - Send It - Tend It & Track

Chapter 1 – A Short History of the Science of Happiness

"All models are wrong, but some are useful."

—*George Box*

The science of happiness and fulfillment is its own river – always moving, sometimes clear, sometimes muddy. It keeps moving.

New studies are published. Old findings are refined or challenged. By the time you read this, some of what we "know" today will have been extended or adjusted. This chapter isn't final answer. It's a map of how we got here and what's reasonably solid. Science evolves. Take what's useful as a guide rather than a rigid rulebook.

From "What's Wrong?" to "What's Working?"

For most of the 20th century, psychology focused on disorders, trauma, and deficits. A "good life" was defined as the absence of illness. That shifted when researchers like Norman Bradburn and Ed Diener started measuring **subjective well-being (SWB)**—how people experience and evaluate their lives (Diener, 1984; Diener et al., 1985, 1999). SWB has three components: **life satisfaction**, a cognitive judgment about one's life as a whole ("All things considered, how satisfied am I with my life?"); **positive affect**, the frequency and intensity of pleasant emotions (joy, gratitude, interest, contentment); and **negative affect**, the frequency and intensity of unpleasant emotions (sadness, anger, anxiety, guilt).

C.A.S.T.
Curiosity - Aim - Send It - Tend It & Track

This matters for leaders because you can be "successful" by external measures and still score low on SWB. Different seasons naturally bring different profiles—for example, high life satisfaction and high negative affect during a crisis. When we refer to well-being in this book, we're mostly talking about subjective well-being over time—the background climate of your life, not momentary mood spikes. "Happiness" may show up occasionally as shorthand, but our real interest is how your leadership life feels to live. The principle underlying SWB was simple but powerful: treat how life feels as something you can measure and learn from. This created reliable ways to compare well-being across people, places, and time. It wasn't perfect—early work relied heavily on self-report surveys and Western samples—but it was a start.

The Rise of Positive Psychology

In the late 1990s and early 2000s, Martin Seligman and Mihaly Csikszentmihalyi argued that psychology had over-focused on problems and needed to study what helps people function well: strengths and virtues, meaning and purpose, engagement and relationships (Seligman & Csikszentmihalyi, 2000).

We saw larger global surveys of happiness and life satisfaction, more longitudinal studies and a wave of simple interventions—gratitude practices, kindness exercises, strengths spotting—that showed small but real effects (Lyubomirsky, 2007; Seligman et al., 2005). Positive psychology normalized an important idea: well-being can be cultivated. Some corners of the movement drifted into overhype—small effects sold as magic solutions, or "be positive" messaging used to gloss over real structural problems. The takeaway for leaders: see it as a useful expansion of the lens. We now study what helps people and systems work well, not only what breaks.

C.A.S.T.
Curiosity - Aim - Send It - Tend It & Track

Life Evaluation and Daily Experience

As research matured, it separated two questions people often blend: "How do you rate your life overall?" (life evaluation) and "How does your life feel day to day?" (experienced well-being).

The drivers aren't identical. Money tends to matter more for life evaluation than daily mood, especially at lower income levels (Kahneman & Deaton, 2010; Kahneman, 2011). Relationships consistently support both (House et al., 1988; Holt-Lunstad et al., 2010; Waldinger & Schulz, 2023). Unemployment or poor-quality work can be especially damaging to both (Lucas et al., 2004).

You can build a life that looks impressive on paper yet feels hollow each day. Or you can build a life that feels rich and connected day to day, even if you've stepped off prestige tracks. Sight Casting asks you to pay attention to both—the story you tell about your life and the felt experience of living it.

Beyond Pleasure: Hedonic and Eudaimonic Well-Being

Hedonic well-being is feeling good: pleasure, enjoyment, comfort, low distress. Eudaimonic well-being is living well: meaning, purpose, growth, values alignment. They overlap, but they're not the same. You can have comfort without meaning. You can have a meaningful life that's overloaded and joyless. Research on eudaimonic well-being—purpose, growth, positive relationships, autonomy—reminded us that "being happy" isn't only about feeling good. It's about living in a way that feels right and worthwhile (Ryan & Deci, 2001; Keyes, 2007). We're concerned with the blend: enough hedonic well-being that life includes real joy, rest, and pleasure, and enough eudaimonic well-being that life feels meaningful, values-aligned, and aimed toward impact.

Peak and Optimal Experience

Csikszentmihalyi's work on **flow** added another dimension: what it feels like to be absorbed in an activity—challenged, focused, and engaged to the point you lose track of time (Csikszentmihalyi, 1990). Flow shows up when skills are matched to a challenge, feedback is immediate, and self-consciousness drops away.

Related work on **peak experiences**—intense moments of awe, connection, or transcendence—reinforced patterns many of us recognize (Maslow, 1964). These brief, powerful moments bring a **sense of connection** (to others, nature, something larger), a **feeling of timelessness**, and a **sense that "this is what matters."**

While peak experiences are short and emotionally intense, flow is usually a sustained state of focused engagement. They can occur together, and both often involve stretch, craft, connection, or contribution. Many people's best memories are about doing, not consuming (Van Boven & Gilovich, 2003).

These states aren't everyday occurrences, but they serve as **compass points**—moments when values and strengths are fully engaged. They tend to arise in contexts that reflect what you care about most: leading through a difficult problem, serving on a mission-driven board, or being with family in a way that feels profoundly right.

The goal is less to accumulate peak experiences and more to understand where and why they happen for you. That insight helps shape your roles, commitments, and environment so that engagement and meaning are more frequent—and your impact comes from the parts of you that feel most alive.

An Evolving Field: What's Changing Now

In recent years we've gotten better methods—long-term panel studies, brain imaging, big data—that add both rigor and nuance (Kahneman, 2011; Diener et al., 2010). The work has also integrated more with adjacent fields like economics, organizational behavior, and health sciences. There's been more attention to context: culture, inequality, job quality, and the social structures that shape well-being (Henrich et al., 2010; Oishi & Westgate, 2021). Researchers have gotten clearer about individual differences—personality, age, and life stage all influence what works for whom (Roberts et al., 2006; Carstensen, 2006; Charles & Carstensen, 2010).

The upshot is simple: this is a serious, cumulative field with robust themes, but it's also provisional and improving. Think of it the way you think about good market data or risk models: helpful, directional, and always open to updating.

Western happiness research is one river, not the only one. Long before surveys and brain scans, other traditions were wrestling with what it means to live well. Stoic philosophers emphasized virtue and the discipline of attention. Buddhist and Eastern contemplative traditions explored the impact of suffering when one clings too tightly to roles, outcomes, or status.

I'm not a scholar or teacher of those paths. This book doesn't try to synthesize them. But it's worth noticing that when you put older traditions next to newer science, themes rhyme. I'll mostly stay in my lane—leaders, research, and lived experience—but those echoes are there if you choose to explore them more deeply.

Learning from Others, Then Finding Your Own Cast: The Lefty Kreh Principle

In fly fishing, there are traditional "rules" about how you're supposed to cast. And then there's Lefty Kreh.

Lefty is widely regarded as one of the most influential casters and fly fishers ever. I was fortunate to meet him on several occasions, and I had the great pleasure—and humiliation—of taking a lesson from him. As critical as he was of my cast, I enjoyed and admired him for many reasons. He learned from others and broke a lot of traditional rules. He experimented. He developed techniques that suited his body, environment, and goals. Many of his once-unorthodox approaches became standard teaching.

That's a useful way to think about both the science of happiness and leadership. Start by leveraging what works for many. Use the research and patterns as your starting kit—the way you learn the basic cast. Then get honest about your own reality. Pay attention to how your temperament, history, role, and life stage shape what works for you. Experiment and adapt. Try new practices, structures, and mindsets, and when something reliably helps you move toward both impact and happiness, keep it—even if it doesn't look like the "standard form." And share what you learn. When you find an approach that works, celebrate it and pass it along. You may be the Lefty Kreh for someone else—showing them an effective way to cast that doesn't fit old templates.

How to Use This Book (and This Science)

This book relies on the available science and the useful patterns I've seen in leaders' lives. By the time it's in your hands, the river of research will have moved, and you will have changed as well. The point is to give you tools, themes, and a map so you can cast your own way—informed by what tends to work, grounded in values and context, and adjusted as insights rise to the surface.

Decades of cognitive science show that human working memory is limited. Early research suggested a capacity of seven items (Miller, 1956). More recent work indicates the limit is often closer to three to five elements, especially when information is complex or unfamiliar (Cowan, 2001). When leaders are overwhelmed with too many ideas, comprehension and recall suffer—a pattern documented in cognitive load theory (Sweller, 1988).

For this reason, this book presents ideas in small, memorable groupings. And, at the end of each of the four major sections, the most important two to six ideas are summarized. The toolkit includes short actions in a one-page *Field Checklist*, designed to be used in real-world leadership moments, reinforcing learning through simplicity and practical application. You can find a printable version of all the tools at SightCastingConsulting.com or SightCastBook.com.

I suggest reading this in at least four or five sittings with time between. Along the way, you'll find short exercises embedded in chapters. I encourage you to pause to answer them. Those moments of reflection are where this book will do most of its work.

In the next chapter, you'll look at what this evolving science says about the main levers of happiness and fulfillment, so you can choose where to cast with greater confidence.

C.A.S.T.
Curiosity - Aim - Send It - Tend It & Track

Chapter 2 – What The Research Tells Us

"The best way to increase happiness is to control the ingredients of happiness, and the main ingredients are not money but social relationships, challenging and meaningful work, and health."

—Ed Diener

Now that you've seen how the field evolved, we can turn to the more practical question: what the science says—and what it doesn't. This chapter is about where we are now: what the research on happiness and fulfillment reliably supports, what it only tentatively suggests, and where you should be careful not to overinterpret.

Think of this as a leader's briefing on the science of well-being:

- What's solid enough to influence how you design your life and leadership

- What's more tentative and should be held lightly

- Where the field simply doesn't know yet

The goal is not to turn you into a researcher. It's to give you enough clarity to Sight Cast more wisely—to decide where to put your time, energy, and attention based on good, not perfect, information.

C.A.S.T.
Curiosity - Aim - Send It - Tend It & Track

Set-Point Theory, Genetics, and Circumstances: Your Baseline, Not Your Fate

One of the most popular ideas to move from academia into pop culture is set-point theory: the claim that each of us has a relatively stable baseline level of happiness we tend to return to after positive or negative events. Some people are naturally more upbeat, while others are more prone to anxiety (Lykken & Tellegen, 1996).

This set point is influenced by genetics and personality. Many people return to a baseline after major events (Brickman & Campbell, 1971; Brickman et al., 1978; Diener et al., 1999). Early interpretations by Lyubomirsky and colleagues suggested ~50% of variance in happiness is explained by genetics, 10% by life circumstances, and 40% by "intentional activities." The numbers were more illustrative than exact, but they stuck.

More cautiously, research supports a few themes. There is stability in reported well-being over time; personality traits and genetic factors matter (McCrae & Costa, 1999). Life circumstances—income, health, employment, relationships—affect well-being, especially at the extremes. Intentional activities and habits—how you relate to others, manage your mind, and use time—play a role.

The research does not support that happiness is fixed like eye color, that you can simply "decide" to be happy or that circumstances barely matter (especially for people in poverty or unsafe environments).

For leaders, this matters because it tempers unrealistic expectations, undermines fatalism, and reminds you that creating better conditions makes a difference. You have a happiness range influenced by genetics and temperament. Where you live in that range is affected by circumstances, habits, and how you respond to experiences.

C.A.S.T.
Curiosity - Aim - Send It - Tend It & Track

Hedonic Adaptation and the Limits of "More"

Another robust finding is **hedonic adaptation**: our tendency to get used to changes, good or bad, and drift back toward a baseline. Lottery winners and accident survivors often return to their prior baseline after an initial spike or drop (Brickman et al., 1978). A raise, promotion, or big purchase often produces a short-term bump that fades.

Later research has nuanced this. Major life events (e.g., disability, unemployment, bereavement) can produce long-lasting shifts in well-being (Lucas et al., 2003; Lucas, 2007). Intentional activities and choices (relationships, work, health behaviors) can also move average well-being in durable ways (Lyubomirsky et al., 2005).

People who experience serious setbacks often recover more well-being over time than outsiders predict—though not always entirely. This does not mean circumstances don't matter. It means chasing more—status, money, and recognition—without changing how you live is unlikely to produce durable happiness. Investing in the fundamentals—relationships, health, meaningful work—tends to have more lasting effects.

For leaders, hedonic adaptation is a warning against designing your life around external milestones, assuming each will finally "fix" how you feel. Achievements are moments, not foundations. How you live between achievements—what your days and relationships feel like—carries more weight.

In other words, the riverbed has a shape, but the channel is yours to work with. You have less control over innate mood than over where you place effort and attention.

The Pillars: Relationships, Work, and Community

Across many studies, three domains repeatedly show up as central to well-being: 1) **close relationships; 2) work and purposeful activity; and 3) community and belonging.**

Relationships - High-quality close relationships are among the strongest and most consistent predictors of both happiness and long-term health outcomes. Loneliness and social isolation are strongly linked to worse mental and physical health. (Holt-Lunstad et al., 2015) It's not the *number* of connections that matters most, but the quality: trust, support, and mutual care.

Work - Being unemployed, underemployed, or in persistently poor-quality work is strongly associated with lower well-being. (Lucas et al., 2004) Having work that offers some combination of autonomy, competence, and connection tends to support both happiness and fulfillment. (Deci & Ryan, 2000) People often report high engagement and satisfaction when they feel they are using their strengths and contributing to something they value.

Community - Feeling that you belong somewhere—whether that's a neighborhood, faith community, professional network, or cause—matters for well-being. Civic and community engagement can enhance a sense of meaning and connection, especially when it's aligned with your values and capacity.

For leaders with heavy responsibilities, the key insight isn't novel, but it is non-negotiable. You can't build a fulfilling life on work alone, nor on relationships or community alone. The shape of your happiness and impact will depend on how these domains interact.

Much of this book is about making those interactions more conscious and sustainable.

C.A.S.T.
Curiosity - Aim - Send It - Tend It & Track

Novelty, Peak Moments, and Psychological Richness

One more ingredient has started to get more attention in recent years: how much novelty, exploration, and "psychological richness" your life contains. Beyond comfort and meaning, some care deeply about having a life that feels varied, interesting, and full of stories—travel, new skills, creative risks, time in wild places. (Oishi & Westgate, 2021)

This shows up both in big "peaks"—rare, intense experiences of awe, connection, or flow we touched on earlier—and in smaller, more frequent moments of engagement: trying something new, stretching a skill. Awe in particular—those times you feel small in a good way, whether in nature, art, or prayer—has been linked to greater meaning, humility, and prosocial behavior. It reminds you that life is part of something larger than your current to-do list.

For our purposes, you can think of this as a fourth pillar alongside relationships, meaningful work, and community. **Connection** is about people who know and love you. **Contribution** is work and roles where you matter. **Community** is a sense of belonging to something larger. And **Novelty** is about experiences that stretch you, absorb you, and connect you to something larger than yourself, making your life feel psychologically rich.

Not everyone will weigh this pillar the same way. Some leaders are novelty seekers by temperament; others are more comfort oriented. But if your life has become one long, predictable grind—even in the service of things you value—it's worth asking whether you've quietly starved this part of yourself. Later, in Chapter 14 and in the Toolkit, you'll look at how to design "freshness" and peak experiences into an otherwise demanding life in ways that fit your season and responsibilities.

C.A.S.T.
Curiosity - Aim - Send It - Tend It & Track

Time Use, Attention, and Daily Experience

Beyond big domains of life, the granular details of how you spend time and attention each day have outsized influence on well-being. Experience-sampling studies and time-use diaries keep pointing to a humbling truth: we often misestimate what makes us happier.

Some activities reliably correlate with better momentary well-being: time with people you enjoy, physical activity, time in nature, and engaging work. Others correlate with lower well-being: long commutes and the drag of screens and doom-scrolling.

Attention is another lever. Mind-wandering tracks with lower momentary happiness, while presence—whether demanded or practiced on purpose—improves the felt quality of that same time.

For leaders, this becomes practical. How much of your day is depleting versus nourishing? How often does your attention get chopped into pieces by notifications or multitasking?

Then comes the part that changes something, small adjustments. One example research keeps citing is simple gratitude. Brief practices don't erase all problems, but they reliably tilt attention toward what's working. That shift in focus supports better moods, stronger relationships, and a more grounded sense that your life, as it is, contains good.

Where can you reduce unnecessary grind—poorly designed meetings, habits that create work without value? And where can you amplify sources of joy through brief walks, a conversation that isn't performative, or blocks of focused work?

You can't turn life into a perpetual spa day. But you have more agency than you think. You can design days that feel less like an unending emergency and more like a life-affirming rhythm.

C.A.S.T.
Curiosity - Aim - Send It - Tend It & Track

What About Health?

The evidence is strong that the basics—adequate sleep, consistent movement, and attention to medical realities—improve your capacity for everything else. It's easier to stay patient in conflict, notice opportunities, experience connection, and think clearly under pressure. While health is never fully under your control, ignoring it makes every other lever harder to pull.

Over the years, I've spent considerable time experimenting with exercise, sleep, diet, and supplements. I take several supplements. Some have an impact I can feel. I include others because the science seems strong. My experience suggests supplements can help in certain contexts. Ultimately, health is personal, and I believe physicians should be part of the process. The goal isn't to chase every online hype, but to start with a good diet and make informed, grounded choices that serve your actual body.

Movement deserves special attention—not just for physical health, but as a practice that supports clear thinking. Walking, in particular, offers a double benefit: an accessible exercise that also creates space for reflection and allows thoughts to percolate. As Nietzsche observed, "All truly great thoughts are conceived by walking" (Nietzsche, 1889). Whether it's a morning walk before the day begins or an afternoon break from screens, movement can be both a health practice and a thinking practice.

In this book, we'll treat health as a background condition you can influence, not as a contest or a new standard to fail. This is not a health handbook, and I'm not qualified to prescribe specific regimen. If you want to go deeper, there are plenty of other resources. What I can offer is how these basics show up in my life and leadership as an illustration of why they matter.

C.A.S.T.
Curiosity - Aim - Send It - Tend It & Track

Field Story: Movement and Mood

I've always been a runner—not particularly competitive, but I love running in the woods. For years, it was my primary way to clear my head and burn off stress.

Over time, running became increasingly painful in my hips and lower back. Biking aggravated the same issues. As pain increased and my exercise declined, so did my patience and mood. It took me a long time to realize I had to stop. I tried shorter runs, fewer days, more stretching, different shoes. I did the tour: physical therapy, sports medicine, imaging, massage. The message from the experts was: put off major surgery as long as possible.

I remember being genuinely mad—not just at the pain, but at what it seemed to mean. I might never be able to rely on running consistently again. Swimming was one of the few things I could do without making the pain worse. The truth is, I find pool swimming monotonous. I experimented anyway. I swam. I tried Pilates and weightlifting. I didn't love any of them the way I love running, but I noticed something simple and stubborn: **I felt better after I did them.** Not months later—right away. My mood lifted. I was less irritable. The day felt more workable.

Over time, I was able to return to running in moderation. By then a deeper lesson had landed: **it's almost impossible for me to stay in a bad mood after I've exercised.** For me, movement—preferably outside—isn't optional if I care about my own happiness, my patience with others, my effectiveness. I'm not suggesting any specific practice is universal. The point is that your body and health are part of the conditions you're leading within. Improvements—especially around sleep and movement—can change your capacity to show up well. This book focuses on how you aim your life, make decisions, and carry responsibility. All of that is easier if you're not fighting your body the whole way.

C.A.S.T.
Curiosity - Aim - Send It - Tend It & Track

What Research Doesn't Tell You (and How to Read It Wisely)

The science of happiness is powerful and useful, but it comes with limits you need to understand.

No personalized formula. No study can tell you exactly what will make you happiest. Research provides patterns and probabilities about what tends to work for many people, on average. How those play out depends on your personality, history, responsibilities, culture, and values. You're working with a map, not a prescription.

No guarantee for any one intervention. Practices like gratitude, meditation, exercise, or volunteering tend to help many people. They don't work the same way for everyone, and they are not cures for systemic problems like toxic workplaces, injustice, or trauma.

No license to blame individuals for their unhappiness. It's tempting to claim that because science shows a certain path to happiness, anyone who isn't happy simply isn't trying hard enough. This perspective ignores structural barriers, mental health conditions, and the reality that everyone begins from a different starting point. Circumstances matter—especially at the extremes.

No reason to ignore discomfort or difficulty. A life focused only on feeling good in the moment is often low on meaning and growth. Some of what leads to deep fulfillment involves stress, sacrifice, and pain in the short-term. The research on meaning, purpose, and long-term health underscores this. Hedonic and eudaimonic well-being are not the same thing, and you need both.

The most helpful stance is to treat "science" like good gear from a respected fly shop—it's better than going out with no tools and no guidance, but it doesn't fish for you. You still have to learn your own river—your mind, your history, your season—and adapt.

C.A.S.T.
Curiosity - Aim - Send It - Tend It & Track

If we strip away complexity and controversy, a few themes keep surfacing—especially when you translate them into how to design a fulfilling life and a workable approach to leadership.

There are real constraints in the system—temperament, genetics, external conditions, health—but they're not the whole story. You have a happiness range you operate within, and where you live in that range is affected by circumstances, habits, and how you respond to experiences. At the same time, chasing more status, income, or achievement without changing how you live and what you value rarely produces lasting happiness. Hedonic adaptation is real. Achievements are moments, not foundations.

Research also keeps pointing back to a few pillars that deserve proactive care: **relationships, purposeful work, and community.** For some people, **novelty and peak experiences** can amplify those pillars, but they don't replace them. While we tend to think big life decisions drive everything, the felt quality of life is shaped as much by **how you use your time and attention day to day**—what you do, who you're with, and where your mind is.

Specific practices can help too—gratitude, movement, sleep, mindfulness—but they're tools, not magic. They work best when they're embedded in a broader shift toward values-based living, not bolted on as one more thing to optimize.

From a Sight Casting perspective, Chapters 1 and 2 are about understanding the water you're in: what tends to support or undermine human flourishing in general, where the current runs strong enough that you can trust it, and where the map is still being drawn. In the next chapter, you'll turn from "what the research says" to what you exploring your own actually personality and tendences.

C.A.S.T.
Curiosity - Aim - Send It - Tend It & Track

Chapter 3 – Seeing Yourself Clearly

"Until you make the unconscious conscious, it will direct your life and you will call it fate"

—Carl Jung

Two leaders can face the same situation and experience it as two different worlds. One steps into a high-pressure role and feels energized. Another steps into the same level of responsibility and feels a constant hum of anxiety, scanning for what might go wrong. Over time, the first leader builds a career that feels aligned and sustainable. The second achieves just as much—but lacks joy and presence and does not feel that their success belongs to them.

Same river. Different anglers.

This chapter is about understanding the gear you bring to the river—your personality, temperament, and habitual patterns of striving—so you can Sight Cast in ways that fit who you are, not who you think you're "supposed" to be.

You'll look at how common personality tools can be helpful when used well and how the patterns they often manifest in high-responsibility leaders. We will also consider how to leverage this awareness for greater happiness, fulfillment, and impact.

Personality Tools as Maps, Not Verdicts

Many of the leaders I work with have encountered at least one of the major personality frameworks (e.g., MBTI, Hogan, DiSC, Enneagram) often used as practical maps of tendencies rather than strict diagnoses (Briggs Myers & Myers, 1995; Hogan & Hogan, 2001). For those who have engaged with personality assessments, leverage those insights to deepen your self-understanding; if you haven't recently, consider exploring an inexpensive online option or gathering feedback from trusted peers and managers using a few targeted questions.

Keep in mind that the output from personality tools can become office buzzwords or excuses ("I'm just a [type], that's why I do this"). Used poorly, they stereotype and limit. Used well, they act as maps of tendencies, not a verdict on who you are or what you're allowed to become.

Each of these tools is really just a flashlight aimed at a few core things: how you see the world, what motivates you, how you respond under stress, and where you tend to overuse your strengths until they quietly turn into liabilities.

You don't have to buy into any one system as *the* truth. The questions that matter are simpler than that. Does this framework help you recognize patterns in how you think, feel, and act? Does it help you see what you default to under pressure? Does it help you notice the ways your "strengths" sometimes get in your own way?

If the answer is yes, it's useful. If it starts to feel like a tight box—or worse, a weapon—it's not being used well.

An Assessment Worth Taking

If you haven't taken a formal personality assessment lately, here are a couple of simple moves you can make that cost nothing and will likely tell you a lot about how your cast is landing.

Start with an internal check. Consider these questions honestly: Do you achieve things but not feel satisfied? Are you physically present but mentally absent? Do you say yes when you mean no? Do you rest but not feel rested? Do your relationships feel transactional? Are you waiting for permission to enjoy your life? Do you scan for problems even during moments meant for pleasure? Do you feel "on the hook" for outcomes you can't fully control?

If several of these questions hit hard, your patterns may be running you rather than serving you. Pay attention to which ones resonate most—they often point to your signature pattern of striving.

Then ask trusted colleagues, mentors, or even friends for candid observations. You can keep it simple with questions like, "What do you see as my greatest strengths when I'm at my best?" or "Where do you think I could be more effective or impactful?" You might also ask, "What's one thing I do that consistently helps—or hinders—our team or project?" or "When have you seen me most energized and alive? When have you seen me most drained?"

Their answers can be an unusually clear mirror. They show you how your "operating system" lands with other people, and they complement what you're learning through self-reflection. The combination of internal experience and external observation gives you a more complete picture of your patterns—and where they might be costing you fulfillment.

C.A.S.T.
Curiosity - Aim - Send It - Tend It & Track

Patterns of Striving in High-Responsibility Leaders

Regardless of which framework you use, certain patterns show up repeatedly in leaders with heavy loads. Most leaders recognize some mix of these in themselves. If you're familiar with tools like the Enneagram (Riso & Hudson, 1999), you may see echoes of types like the Reformer, the Achiever, or the Loyal Skeptic here—but you don't need that language for this to be useful.

The first pattern is over-functioning and control. These leaders are always scanning for what might go wrong, stepping in to fix things before others have a chance, and taking responsibility for everyone's outcomes and even their emotions. The upside is that things get done and standards are upheld. The effectiveness cost is exhaustion, resentment, and other people's underdevelopment. The fulfillment cost is that you never feel like you can truly rest, which means you're never fully present for joy.

The second pattern of striving is over-accommodating and harmony-seeking. Here the leader has a hard time saying no, avoids conflict—especially with people they value—and routinely takes on more than is sustainable to prevent disappointment or discord. The upside is strong relationships, loyalty, and cohesion. The effectiveness cost is blurred boundaries, quiet burnout, and indirectness when clarity is needed (Maslach & Leiter, 2016). The fulfillment cost is that you lose touch with what you want, and your life becomes a series of responses to others' needs rather than choices aligned with your own values.

The third pattern is achievement-as-identity. There is a deep drive to succeed, often formed early in life. Self-worth becomes closely linked to performance and external validation. Even big wins don't feel satisfying for long; the bar moves almost as soon as it's cleared. The upside is ambition, stamina, and results. The effectiveness cost is a sense of emptiness after achievements, difficulty resting, and relationships becoming more instrumental than genuine. The fulfillment cost is that success feels hollow because you're always chasing the next milestone, which means you never arrive.

The fourth pattern is over-analysis and caution. These leaders feel a strong need to understand all angles before acting. They find it hard to make decisions under uncertainty and may withdraw under pressure or ruminate instead of moving. The upside is sound judgment and real risk awareness. The cost is paralysis, missed opportunities, and mental spirals that drain energy. The fulfillment cost is that you live more in your head than in your life, and rumination replaces experience.

Most leaders carry some blend of these patterns. None of them are inherently good or bad. The real issue is rigidity: when you only have one way to respond, regardless of context, and you keep using it long after the situation calls for something different.

From a Sight Casting perspective, your patterns of striving shape what you notice and what you ignore. They also influence when you tend to over-cast—taking on too many commitments or reaching for too much control—and where you tend to under-cast, through avoidances and neglected areas of life. Seeing these patterns clearly is the first step to choosing differently.

Field Note: Over-Responsibility and Integrity
Like many of my peers, I attribute much of my success to preparation and hard work. I feel a deep responsibility to ensure my team and partners are treated fairly and can provide for their families. Consequently, I anticipate risk and do everything possible to avoid negative outcomes. This intent can lead to behavior perceived as "trying to control everything."

Throughout this book, I reference 'assuming positive intent' and 'leading with a recommendation.' I would like to think these models were constructed out of personal strength. The opposite is true.

My personality profile shows strong Enneagram Type 8 characteristics—a pattern marked by a need for control, protection of others, and resistance to vulnerability. Type 8s are often called 'The Challenger' or 'The Protector': we're energized by taking charge, we're highly attuned to power dynamics and injustice, and we instinctively move toward conflict rather than away from it. At our best, we're decisive, protective, and empowering. At our worst, we're domineering, distrustful, and unable to let others lead.

It is not always in my nature to assume positive intent. Perhaps it's because I was mugged as a teenager or worked for managers who used me as a scapegoat. Regardless, assuming positive intent took deep personal work. Similarly, the "leading with recommendations" framework grew from my tendency to "jump in" and solve every problem myself.

I offer these insights for two reasons. First, our greatest strengths, when exaggerated, become weaknesses. In my case, seeking control prevents others from growing and keeps me from hearing better solutions. Second, understanding and managing our weaknesses drives value for everyone. Multiple team members have shared that our culture of assuming positive intent was a career highlight. I've also seen organizations deliver stronger results—clearer decisions, faster execution, and less escalation—after adopting the "leading with recommendations" framework as a shared norm.

All of that started with simple, often uncomfortable curiosity about my own patterns.

C.A.S.T.
Curiosity - Aim - Send It - Tend It & Track

Self-Awareness as a Lever

Why does any of this matter for **happiness and fulfillment**, not just effectiveness? Because your inherent patterns profoundly shape your experience. They influence how you experience your responsibilities: do you consistently feel "on the hook," or do you experience appropriate accountability? Do you perceive others as disappointments to manage, or as partners to develop? They shape how you relate to joy, rest, and connection: can you be fully present for moments of pleasure and meaning, or is your mind constantly scanning for the next problem? Do you feel permission to genuinely enjoy what you've built, or are you always compelled to move on to what's next? And they affect how you interpret discomfort: do you see it as a sign to stop (avoiding fracture at all costs), a signal to push harder (to prove your worth), or simply as information—a cue to check if you're aligned with your values?

Self-awareness doesn't fundamentally alter your basic wiring; instead, it transforms your relationship to it. This kind of self-awareness is also at the heart of the **Acceptance and Commitment Therapy (ACT)** tools you'll explore later: noticing thoughts and urges without automatically obeying them and choosing your next move from your values rather than from habit.

Using Tools Without Letting Them Use You

If you already know your Enneagram, MBTI, Hogan, or DiSC profile, there are a few constructive ways to use that information.

First, read the "under stress" sections carefully. Most instruments spell out how you tend to behave when pressure rises. Pay attention to what you do more of—usually overdriving your strengths—and what you do less of, like stopping listening, excluding others, or neglecting your own need for rest. Then ask:

C.A.S.T.
Curiosity - Aim - Send It - Tend It & Track

How does this affect my happiness and fulfillment? And how does it impact my effectiveness and my relationships?

Second, ask trusted people if the descriptions ring true. Invite one or two colleagues, your partner, or a friend to respond to questions like, "Where do you see this in me?" and "Where do you see me getting in my own way?" You may feel defensive at first but try to come back to the data they give you. That outside perspective is part of learning to read the river more accurately.

Third, identify one "signature overuse." Most high-capacity leaders have at least one pattern they lean on too hard—over-controlling, over-accommodating, over-achieving, over-analyzing. Name yours, then simply observe it for a few weeks. The goal isn't to eliminate it overnight; it's to notice when it shows up, especially when it isn't necessary or helpful.

Fourth, experiment with a small counter-move. If you over-control, delegate one task with clear expectations and give someone space to struggle and learn. If you over-accommodate, practice one clean, respectful "no" this week. If you over-achieve, protect a block of time for something meaningful that isn't "productive." If you over-analyze, set a strict time limit on one decision and commit to the best choice you can with what you know. You're not trying to become a different person—you're testing what happens when you slightly change how you cast.

Finally, revisit your profile as your life changes. As roles, responsibilities, and life evolve, different parts of your personality come forward. Re-reading old results with fresh eyes can surface new insights: "This used to be adaptive; now it's more costly," or "That strength I minimized might be exactly what I need more of now." The person reading this book isn't the same person you were ten years ago. Both the river and the angler have changed.

C.A.S.T.
Curiosity - Aim - Send It - Tend It & Track

Personality, Stress, and Flourishing

Your personality shapes how you experience stress and opportunity, but it doesn't determine your capacity for happiness or fulfillment. Some temperaments may be more prone to rumination, over-commitment, or conflict-avoidance. Those patterns can make the path more complex, but they don't close it.

Here's what's at stake: your personality patterns shape whether you experience your life as something you're living or something you're enduring. They determine whether your achievements feel meaningful or empty, and whether you can be present for the people who matter most—or whether you're always half-somewhere-else, managing the next thing.

The leaders I work with who report the highest levels of fulfillment aren't necessarily the ones with the "easiest" temperaments. They're the ones who've done the work to see their patterns clearly and choose when to follow them and when to set them aside. They've learned to distinguish between the voice of their pattern ("You need to control this or it will fall apart") and the voice of their values ("What matters most to me right now?").

This chapter focused on Curiosity at the individual level: who you are, how you move through the world, and what that means for sustainable, meaningful leadership. The goal isn't to eliminate your patterns or become someone else. It's to see yourself clearly enough that you can choose when to lean into your natural tendencies and when to consciously do something different—not because you "should," but because it serves the life you want to live.

Next, you'll zoom out to the river itself—your life stages, transitions, and the shocks that change the waters you're in.

C.A.S.T.
Curiosity - Aim - Send It - Tend It & Track

Chapter 4 – Life Stages, Transitions, and the Shocks of Life

"No man ever steps in the same river twice, for it's not the same river and he's not the same man."
—Heraclitus

The river of your life is not a static pond. It flows.

Sometimes the water is slow and glassy. Sometimes it's fast and technical. Sometimes a storm that is many miles upstream turns what looked like a predictable run into a muddy torrent. This chapter is about staying curious about that evolution and learning to adjust how you cast, instead of trying to fish the same way in fundamentally different water. Beneath the metaphor, we're really talking about three elements:

1. **Life stages** – the relatively predictable shifts in roles and responsibilities.

2. **Major transitions** – the intense passages that reconfigure your life.

3. **Shocks** – the ruptures that arrive without your consent.

Underneath all of that is a deeper question: how to stay anchored in values and adjust so you can keep leading, caring, and living meaningfully—even as the river keeps changing.

C.A.S.T.
Curiosity - Aim - Send It - Tend It & Track

Life Stages: Different Waters, Different Fish

Each broad stage of life brings its own mix of demands, constraints, and opportunities. What supports your well-being at one stage may be unsustainable, or simply irrelevant, at another. Curiosity here means regularly asking, "Given the water I'm in now, what actually works?"

You can think of the arc in three movements: early career building, mid-career peak responsibility, and later career legacy and transition (Levinson, 1978; Bridges, 2004). These stages look different across gender and culture—timing, expectations, and constraints vary—but the pattern of evolving demands holds.

Early Career / Building Phase (roughly 20s–30s)

In the early stretch, the current tends to run fast. The main work is establishing competence and proving worth. You are building a professional and financial foundation, often by saying yes to a lot: long hours, travel, stretch projects, moves.

That intensity can be exciting and formative. It also carries predictable risks. Burnout is common when ambition runs ahead of any clear boundary. Identity can fuse almost entirely with work: "Who am I beyond my job?" Health, friendships, and hobbies are easy to neglect in the name of hustle.

What helps at this stage is not perfect balance, but a few anchors. Learning goals and skill growth can make the grind feel purposeful. Mentors and peer groups can help normalize turbulence. Basic boundaries—sleep that is good enough, regular movement, and at least a few relationships that get real time—keep the engine from seizing. This is a good time to experiment without treating missteps as a verdict on your worth.

C.A.S.T.
Curiosity - Aim - Send It - Tend It & Track

From a Sight Casting lens, many leaders learn to cast in this season mostly by sheer effort. That can work for a while. But the same drive that propels can quietly become a liability if you never get curious about how your water is changing and adjust your cast.

Mid-Career / Peak Responsibility (roughly 30s–50s)

For many leaders reading this, this is the water you're standing in now. Professionally, your scope is wide: P&L responsibility, teams, boards, investors, and complex stakeholder landscapes. At the same time, family responsibilities often peak: young kids, teenagers, or both; sometimes aging parents. Add community roles and board seats, and you have high load, high complexity, and very little slack.

The challenges here are less about one-off crises and more about chronic conditions: a sense of overwhelm and time scarcity; the feeling of being pulled in many directions with no "off" season; losing yourself in roles—operator, parent, partner, child, board member—until you're not sure who is underneath all of those.

What helps in this season is a different kind of ambition. Ruthless prioritization becomes non-optional: a willingness to disappoint some people and say no in service of a deeper yes. Delegation and trust are no longer "nice leadership behaviors"; they are survival strategies. You cannot hold everything personally and remain healthy. Non-negotiable blocks—sleep, movement, time with the handful of people who matter most—move from the margins to the center. Peer forums and trusted circles where you can speak honestly can be more stabilizing than any single self-care tactic. This is the season when leaders realize what got them here won't get them there. Curiosity shifts from "How do I do more?" to "What needs to change for this to be sustainable and meaningful?"

C.A.S.T.
Curiosity - Aim - Send It - Tend It & Track

Later Career / Legacy and Transition (roughly 50s–60s and beyond)

Eventually the river widens again. Roles change. You may find yourself spending more time on mentoring, succession, board work, and governance. Questions of exit, legacy, and "what's next" come into sharper focus. Around you, you see more peers navigating illness, divorce, the loss of parents and friends. Your own energy levels and health may be less predictable.

In this season, identity questions become louder. Who am I without this role, this company, this level of centrality? There can be fear of irrelevance or being "past it," alongside a real desire to contribute without carrying the same heroic load. Daily social contact can shift dramatically as roles and rhythms change.

What seems to help here is proactive, honest planning—not only financial planning, but psychological and social planning for life after the current role. That might include reviving or developing new interests, from hobbies and teaching to service and place-based commitments. Intergenerational relationships that connect across ages (mentoring, grandparenting, community work) often carry a different kind of meaning. And health moves from being a "nice to have" to infrastructure: something you build around, not something you squeeze in.

Seen through the river metaphor, this stage is less about running the most technical rapids and more about choosing where you want to spend your remaining days on the water. Curiosity sounds different now: "If I didn't have to prove anything, what kind of impact would I actually want to have?"

Major Transitions: Navigating the Rapids

Overlapping with broad life stages are specific, often intense transitions. Some you choose; others are chosen for you. Either way, they create rapids: stretches where the current accelerates, the water changes character, and your usual moves may not work.

In the rapids, Curiosity narrows and becomes practical: *What's happening? What matters most right now? What small adjustments will keep me upright?*

Common Rapids

Career transitions are one frequent set of rapids. Stepping into a bigger role—a CEO seat, partnership, C-level job, or major GM position—brings visibility, a steep learning curve, more politics, and a spike of imposter syndrome. Navigation here means designing your own onboarding: clarifying expectations, asking what success looks like in the first 6–12 months, protecting a few non-negotiables (sleep, movement, one or two core relationships), and quickly building a trusted circle—a coach, mentor, and peers who will tell you the truth.

Other transitions come from changing the kind of work you do. Leaving a well-worn path for something more values-aligned—a new industry, a startup, an independent or portfolio career—often mixes fear and genuine creative energy. The work is to be financially realistic about runway and downside, map which skills transfer and which need to be built, be willing to be a beginner again, and have explicit conversations at home about what this move will mean in practice.

Family transitions create a different kind of rapid. The arrival of children reshapes time, energy, and priorities more radically than most anticipate. Profound meaning and joy often coexist with sleep loss, stress, and strain on partnerships. The work is to renegotiate roles explicitly instead of by silent default, lower perfectionism in both parenting and leadership, and accept that some seasons will not be "balanced" in any conventional sense—and can still be aligned with your values.

Later, an empty nest can feel like someone turned down the volume on your life. The house is quieter. There's more space in the calendar. What shows up with that can be grief and loneliness alongside a sense of possibility. Many leaders rediscover or deepen their relationship with a partner or close friends. Interests that were on hold for decades re-emerge. The work in this season is to redefine impact, shifting from day-to-day parenting to more local, mentoring, or community-focused contribution.

One transition that is both common and under-discussed among senior leaders is caring for aging parents. The impact on well-being can be significant: stress, guilt, grief, time pressure, and complex family dynamics, intertwined with deep moments of connection and meaning. Navigating this usually requires clearer communication with siblings than most families are used to, professional help when needed (legal, financial, and care management), and explicit adjustment to your own expectations of yourself at work and at home.

Geographic moves bring their own version of rapids. Relocation disrupts almost every stabilizing structure: social networks, routines, and place-based rituals. Navigation here means rebuilding social and community life as a primary project, not an afterthought. It involves establishing new anchor routines—a gym, a coffee place, a walking route, or a faith community—while intentionally maintaining a small set of old connections.

C.A.S.T.
Curiosity - Aim - Send It - Tend It & Track

The Shocks of Life: When the River Blows Out

In March of 2025, my mom had a stroke.

Nothing in my calendar had room for that. There was no planning cycle, no strategy offsite, no quarterly goals that accounted for it. One day my life had a certain rhythm; the next day, it was gone. For months, I took weekly multi-day trips to see her—in the hospital, then skilled nursing, then assisted living. I juggled work, long drives, medical updates, hard conversations, and emotional weight of watching a parent fight to regain abilities.

Nothing about that season was balanced. I wasn't calmly implementing a well-being plan. I was adjusting fast, and then adjusting again as her situation evolved. Some weeks, the best I could do was get enough sleep to avoid dangerous mistakes and show up fully for the few work conversations that mattered, while letting the rest be "good enough." From the outside, it might have looked like a disruption to normal life. From the inside, it felt like my real life had just made itself known, and everything else had to flex around it.

This kind of transition doesn't fit neatly into work/life diagrams. It forces questions you may have been able to postpone: What does it mean to be a good son, sibling, parent, spouse, and leader when there isn't enough of you to go around? Where can you lower the bar without losing integrity?

My mom's stroke was one version of something many people experience: a shock that blows the river out. Some changes you see coming. Others hit like a flash flood—the sudden loss of a loved one or relationship, a serious diagnosis, a financial crisis, or trauma that shatters assumptions about safety, fairness, or control. These aren't just transitions; they're ruptures. They challenge your story about who you are and what you can count on.

C.A.S.T.
Curiosity - Aim - Send It - Tend It & Track

There are no efficient shortcuts through this kind of season. Grief and processing take time. Professional support like therapists and counselors can be essential. This is not the time to try to do life alone; relationships and support become part of the survival kit.

In that season with my mom, values and the framework in this book weren't optimization tools; they were survival tools. Values gave me a way to decide where to be when I couldn't be everywhere. Sleep, some exercise and a few trusted relationships kept me functional. Some transitions don't invite you to fine-tune your life. They demand that you reorder it.

Shocks bring a brutal kind of clarity. They strip away noise and force tough questions about what matters. Practices and values don't erase pain, but they can frame small decisions: What is the kind thing to do today? Where can I lower the bar and practice self-compassion? What is the next step, not a full recovery plan?

In these seasons, the goal often shifts from "thriving" to remaining intact enough to care, to decide, and to eventually rebuild.

Recalibration: You Are Not the Same Angler

Across stages, transitions, and shocks, one thing is constant: you are changing. The person reading this book is not the same person who took their first leadership role, navigated parenthood, or faced their first major loss. That's not just poetic; it has direct implications for happiness, fulfillment, and sustainable impact.

Values shift in emphasis. Autonomy that once felt paramount may make room for stewardship or legacy. Your definition of impact may change. Tactics that worked in your thirties may be misaligned in your fifties.

I once worked with a leader who, in front of a large group, declared that health had never been an important value to him. When he took a values assessment, it scored at the bottom of his list—and his behavior confirmed it. But as a dad of young children, something shifted. If he wanted to be there for his kids, he needed to change his lifestyle. He decided to put health in his top five values, even though for his entire life it had ranked nowhere near the top. That wasn't weakness or inconsistency. It was recalibration.

What was adaptive in one season—relentless drive, hyper responsibility, heroic contribution—can quietly become harmful in the next, showing up as an inability to delegate, health erosion, or absence from relationships. Treating your old playbook as non-negotiable is a reliable way to burn out, hollow out, or both.

This is why curiosity driven reflection isn't a luxury; it's an operational necessity. After big events—a liquidity moment, a health scare, a loss, a relocation—it's worth asking: Do my old values still fit? Have my priorities shifted without my choices catching up? When the old map is out of date, values become your compass for what to protect, what to let go, and what to rebuild.

Sleep and energy may need more protection during peak responsibility years. Relationships may need rebuilding after intense career sprints or after kids leave home. Work design may need to shift from front stage to back stage as you move into legacy focused roles. Inner tools—like ACT skills you'll see later—matter when external conditions are hardest to control.

You can't control the river. You can stop pretending it isn't changing. Here are some practical moves: anticipate predictable transitions earlier than you think needed; normalize the learning curve; revisit values after big events; adjust commitments prior to

C.A.S.T.
Curiosity - Aim - Send It - Tend It & Track

a crisis; and seek support instead of performing heroics. Peers, family, coaches, and therapists are part of a sane strategy, not evidence you're weak. Leaders who last are not the ones who try to carry everything alone.

Why This Matters for Your Happiness and Leadership

For leaders with heavy loads, it's easy to treat happiness and fulfillment as something you'll get to "once things calm down." They rarely do.

If you try to live this season with last season's strategy, three things happen. Your well-being erodes in ways that are initially invisible but eventually undeniable. Your leadership quality declines: reactivity increases, patience shrinks, decisions narrow to what's urgent rather than what's important. Your sense of integrity gets strained as your actions your stated values diverge.

Recognizing the evolving river is not indulgence. It is stewardship—of your own capacity to keep showing up, of the people you lead who are watching how you navigate your own transitions, and of the systems and organizations that depend on you remaining effective, humane, and accountable over time.

Exercise: Name Your Current Life Stage

Take a moment to name where you are right now. Which life stage best describes your current season—building, peak responsibility, or legacy and transition? Are you in the middle of a major transition (a new role, family change, or geographic move)? Are you navigating a shock that reordered your life? Write down one sentence that captures your current reality, then ask: *Given the water I'm in now, what needs to change for this to be sustainable and meaningful?*

Key Takeaways from Part I: Curiosity

Before you can cast with intention, you have to see the water clearly—the conditions you're in, the patterns you bring, and the stage of the river you're navigating. Otherwise, you default to **over-casting for achievement** instead of aiming at impact. If there were two key insights from Part I, they are:

1. **You can influence your happiness and fulfillment by focusing on the pillars:** The research is clear. relationships, meaningful work, community, and novelty matter more than chasing the next milestone. Supporting all of this is your health; without physical and mental well-being, it is nearly impossible to show up fully for the people and work that matter most. Where you place your time and attention day-to-day shapes the felt quality of your life.

2. **Your personality patterns shape what you notice, what you ignore, and where you over- or under-cast:** Whether you tend toward over-functioning, over-accommodating, achievement-as-identity, or analysis-as-default, seeing these tendencies clearly is the first step to choosing differently. Use feedback from peers or a personality assessment to identify your signature "overuse"—then experiment with a small countermove.

Looking Ahead: The Changing River

In the next part, you'll be more deliberate with those clues as we turn raw curiosity into something you can steer by. You'll turn more explicitly toward Aim: your values, your definition of impact, and the shift from achievement for its own sake to a life that feels both meaningful and sustainable given the river you're in now, so you stop over-casting in the wrong water.

C.A.S.T.
Curiosity - Aim - Send It - Tend It & Track

PART II: AIM

Choosing Your Direction and Values

You've been gathering clues: moments that quietly pull at you, flashes of envy, stories you never tire of telling. Part I was about noticing—letting the river of your life come into view. Now, you'll be more deliberate. Part II is about **Aim**. Not a five-year plan, but the underlying direction of your life—what you stand for, what you want your presence to change, and what "a good use of yourself" truly means. You'll surface your core values, clarify impact in your work, relationships, and community, and explore the shift from achievement to meaningful, sustainable contribution.

Think of Part II as moving from "I'm curious" to "I'm choosing". Without an honest sense of Aim, you're left reacting to currents you didn't choose. In these pages, you'll put language to the kind of life that would feel like a good cast of you.

C.A.S.T.
Curiosity - **Aim** - Send It - Tend It & Track

Chapter 5 – What are you Really Aiming At?

"If a man knows not to which port he sails, no wind is favorable."

—*Seneca*

You've already built a life of significant achievement. You've climbed the ladder, delivered results, and earned your place. Yet, for many leaders, there comes a point where the relentless pursuit of the next achievement starts to feel hollow. The satisfaction is fleeting, the energy required is immense, and the question begins to surface:

Is this all there is?

You've seen why more achievement doesn't automatically produce more happiness; and how your own defaults under load shape your experience. Across the next three chapters, you'll work through three related questions:

- **What matters now?** (Values)

- **What am I trying to change in the world, in this season?** (Impact)

- **Who am I if the river bends hard?** (Identity)

This chapter is about the first and most foundational of those: **values**—your answer to "What matters now?"

C.A.S.T.
Curiosity – **Aim** - Send It – Tend It & Track

Before we talk about the change you want to create "out there," or who you'll be when your roles and circumstances shift, we need to ground you in the values you want to live by *here and now*.

By the end of this chapter, you'll have a small set of core values—the **qualities of action** and ways of being that you want to carry into the rest of Part II and into the work in Parts III and IV.

Values: Your Internal Compass

Back in the Introduction section, we defined values as chosen directions—qualities of action you care about living out, not boxes you can check and be done. Here, we're going to make those values concrete enough to steer by.

Think of them as your **internal compass**. When you're aligned with your values, you feel a sense of purpose, integrity, and vitality. When you're out of alignment, you feel drained, conflicted, or resentful.

Some common values include:

- **Integrity**: Honesty, ethical conduct, trustworthiness.
- **Growth**: Learning, personal development, continuous improvement.
- **Connection**: Belonging, intimacy, strong relationships.
- **Contribution**: Making a difference, service, generosity.
- **Autonomy**: Freedom, independence, self-direction.
- **Courage**: Facing challenges, speaking truth, taking risks.
- **Well-being**: Health, vitality, balance.

Many leaders carrying heavy responsibility have a strong sense of values, but those values often stay unarticulated and unexamined. They operate in the background—quietly guiding decisions without being consciously named. The trouble with implicit values is how easily they get overridden. External pressures creep in: the demands of the job and the pull of cultural norms. Habitual patterns take over: the default ways you've always operated, even when they no longer serve you. And achievement becomes its own gravity, pulling you toward the next milestone. Stoic philosophy calls this "living by whim" rather than by principle. Without a named set of values, you aren't sailing toward a port; you are simply being blown by the winds of other people's expectations.

Exercise: Uncovering Your Core Values

Before we go further, pause and reflect. Use a journal or the worksheets in the toolkit to answer these questions honestly:

- What truly matters to you, deep down?
- What qualities of action do you want to embody in your work, relationships, and community?
- When you look back on your life, what did you stand for?
- What makes you feel most engaged and purposeful?
- What makes you feel drained, resentful, or out of integrity? (The opposite of these often points to a core value.)

Often, **4–5 core values** are enough to provide a powerful compass. As you continue through Part II—and into the tools and practices of Parts III and IV—keep those values in view. They are the thread you'll use to aim your choices and behaviors.

Field Story: Early Life Experience

One of the earliest experiences that truly shaped my values—especially around responsibility and sustainability—came when I was a senior in college and got an opportunity that felt equal parts gift and weight: co-ownership of a small local balloon and promotions business that was struggling to stay afloat. Helium Highs, Inc. didn't need inspiration—it needed oxygen.

That season taught me what responsibility looks like in the wild. I learned to bootstrap the unromantic way: cut expenses, sell assets, and get out from behind the desk. I hit the streets and talked to customers face to face. I told them the truth about where the business stood, and I shared my plan for turning it around—not as a performance, but as a commitment. Their loyalty and trust didn't just feel good; it created real breathing room. We stemmed the bleeding, hired part-time help, and within six months clawed our way into marginal profitability. Not a victory lap—but a pulse.

Then the river shifted.

In 1989, one of our core product offerings was criticized in the local paper as a risk to marine life. Dr. Frank Schwartz from UNC's Department of Marine Biology warned that helium balloons released at football games were traveling to the Atlantic Ocean, where sea turtles mistook them for jellyfish and ate them.

I could have minimized it or told myself it wasn't my problem. Instead, I called Dr. Schwartz. Not to argue—to learn. I asked him to walk me through what he was seeing and what the downstream consequences looked like. The more I listened, the clearer it became that this wasn't abstract.

I was in a real bind: we were fighting to keep a small business alive, and the practice being criticized was a major source of revenue. Saying no would hurt immediately. After some deep

C.A.S.T.
Curiosity - **Aim** - Send It - Tend It & Track

consideration, I decided to stop supplying balloons for those releases. It cost us. Values that never cost you anything aren't really values—they're preferences.

What I didn't expect was what happened next. The local news community publicized our decision—loudly, and in print. A well-established event promoter reached out and eventually awarded Helium Highs the largest contract we'd ever had.

I don't tell this as a neat "do the right thing and you'll be rewarded" fable. Sometimes doing the right thing just costs you. But that season formed something in me. Responsibility isn't only about commitments and performance; it's about owning downstream effects. Sustainability isn't a slogan you add later; it's part of how you decide what kind of profitable you're willing to be. And I learned—viscerally—that doing the right thing and building a profitable brand aren't mutually exclusive.

From Achievement to What Matters Now

For many leaders, **success has been defined by a clear trajectory of achievement:** promotions, revenue targets, market share, awards, titles. These are important metrics, and they often reflect real competence and hard work.

But a life solely focused on achievement can become a **treadmill**. The goal is always just ahead, and the satisfaction of reaching it is fleeting. Part I showed you some of the psychology behind this: hedonic adaptation. That raises a different kind of question: Given everything I've already accomplished, and everything I know now about how happiness and fulfillment actually work, **what is worth aiming at in this season of my life?**

C.A.S.T.
Curiosity – **Aim** - Send It – Tend It & Track

A Pattern Many Leaders Recognize: The "Striver's Curse"

Harvard's Arthur Brooks calls one common pattern among high achievers the "striver's curse": the sense that no amount of success quite feels like enough, and that each win quickly becomes the new baseline. (Brooks, 2019) His work, and others', points to a different set of pillars that support durable happiness:

- Faith or philosophy – some coherent frame for meaning and transcendence, religious or not.
- Family and close friendships – a few relationships of real depth and mutual care.
- Meaningful work– using your strengths in service of something you value.
- Service to others– contributing to people and causes beyond yourself.

For many leaders, Part II of this book is about shifting from the striver's treadmill—more achievement, little lasting satisfaction—toward a portfolio of life that rests more on these pillars. Your values work is how you decide what that portfolio looks like for you now, not in abstract.

Values translate that question into something more concrete. Rather than asking, "What's the next impressive thing I can do?" values invite you to ask: *"What choices, in this chapter, would be a good use of me?"*

Later, you'll apply that lens explicitly to **impact**—to what you want to change in the world. For now, stay close to home: your own life, your relationships, your day-to-day decisions.

The Angler's True Aim: What Matters *for You*

Think about fly fishing. Some anglers are driven by the sheer number of fish they catch. For them, success is a high count. Others are motivated by the size of a single trophy fish—the bigger, the better. Still others care less about the catch itself and are more about spending time with others on the water. And then there are those who are primarily drawn to the environment: the peace of a remote mountain stream, the challenge of the open ocean, or the quiet beauty of a lake at dawn.

Each of these motivations is valid. No single goal is inherently more important than another. What matters is what makes the individual angler feel engaged, purposeful, and fulfilled.

Your values work the same way. There's no universal "right" set. Your job isn't to adopt someone else's list—it's to get honest about what truly animates you.

One way in is to look back over the last year and ask: when have you felt most like yourself? What were you doing, and who were you with? Another is to strip away the usual scaffolding—titles, metrics, external recognition—and ask what you would still care deeply about if none of that were on the table. And a third is to imagine your calendar suddenly cleared and notice what you'd move toward, not just what you'd run from.

You're the one standing in your stretch of river. You decide what "a good day" looks like there.

Linking What Matters to Your Leadership

It's tempting to treat this work as "personal" and separate from "real" leadership issues. But for employers and organizations, the values-alignment and well-being of their leaders is not a soft perk; it's what keeps good anglers in the water.

A leader who is burned out, disengaged, or out of alignment with their values becomes **less effective**, they're more prone to poor decision-making, short-term thinking, and reactive leadership. They also become **less accountable**, more likely to cut corners, avoid difficult conversations, or outsource responsibility for their own well-being. And they become **less inspiring**, because it's hard to foster a culture of engagement, resilience, or high performance when you're running on fumes.

Conversely, leaders who are clear about what matters now—who can name their values and make decisions in line with them—tend to be **more effective**, capable of sustained strategic thinking, navigating complexity, and fostering innovation. They're also **more accountable**, taking ownership not just for results, but for the health of the organization and the development of their people. And they're **more inspiring**, modeling resilience, integrity, and a deep commitment to purpose in a way that cultivates a thriving culture.

Doing work on values is not self-indulgent. It's a foundational part of high-impact, sustainable leadership.

The Evolving Self: What Matters *Now* vs. *Then*

Your values are not carved in stone. Over time, through different stages and events, **what matters now** may not be what mattered a decade ago.

This is why the question for this chapter is not "What are my values forever?" but: **"What matters most, to me, *now*, in this season of my life?"**

C.A.S.T.
Curiosity - **Aim** - Send It - Tend It & Track

That means **revisiting values is crucial.** What felt paramount five years ago may have shifted. It means **making real space for reflection.** It means **allowing your definition of "what matters" to evolve**—because that's a sign of growth, not inconsistency.

We will come back to identity and life stages in much more depth in Chapter 7. For now, it's enough to acknowledge *you* are evolving, and your aim needs to reflect the angler you are now, not the one you were two or three chapters of life ago.

Exercise: Your Values for This Season
To make this real, write down your answers to these prompts:

1. **List 4–5 core values** that you captured earlier. Do these feel most resonant for you in this season of your life. If not, consider adjusting.

2. For each, write a **one-sentence description** in your words.

3. For each value, name one concrete behavior that would express that value in your current life and leadership. For example, if the value is Connection, you might say, "I want to be the kind of leader who makes people feel seen and safe to be honest." Then you translate that into action by scheduling 30 minutes of real one-on-one time with each of your direct reports, with no agenda other than listening.

These 4–5 values are the **through-line** you'll carry into the rest of the book. In Chapter 6, you'll ask: *Given what matters now, what am I trying to change in the world, this season?* In Chapter 7: *When the river bends hard—when roles change, when shocks hit—who am I, and how do I stay anchored in these values?*

For now, don't rush ahead. Stand where you are in the river and answer, as honestly as you can: **What matters, to me, right now?**

C.A.S.T.
Curiosity – **Aim** - Send It – Tend It & Track

Chapter 6 – Impact: The Difference You Are Making

"Be ashamed to die until you have won some victory for humanity."

—Horace Mann

"Impact" shows up everywhere—impact investing, impact reports, impact strategies. But when you set the buzzwords aside and ask one simple question—

What difference is my life making, to the people and places I touch?

—most leaders go quiet.

This chapter is about that question. Not the aspirational, "someday" answer. The present-tense lived answer. By the end of this chapter, you should be able to see three things more clearly:

1. Where your impact is already real and healthy.

2. Where impact is real but costly in ways that don't fit your values.

3. Where you want to shift—from achievement for its own sake toward impact you'd be proud to have your kids or closest colleagues describe when you're not in the room.

This isn't about perfection. It's about aim. You can't Sight Cast toward impact if you haven't named what you're trying to change.

C.A.S.T.
Curiosity - **Aim** - Send It - Tend It & Track

Achievement vs. Impact

Achievement is about what you reach. Impact is about what your reach changes.

Achievement is the promotion, the exit, the award, the revenue target. **Impact is what those achievements do to and for other people**—and, just as importantly, what they do to and for you. And to be clear, some achievements absolutely *do* create impact. Hitting a revenue target can fund innovation, stabilize jobs, and improve service for customers. Winning a bid can bring a better solution to a community. Getting the role can put you in position to build a healthier culture. The point isn't that achievement is shallow; it's that it's incomplete as a compass.

Achievement questions tend to be clean and binary: did we hit the number, did we win the bid, did I get the role? They're useful, and in most leadership contexts they're unavoidable. Impact questions widen the frame. If we hit the number, what changed for customers, students, patients, or the community because we did? What changed for the people on this team—their skills, confidence, careers, and families? And what did it cost to produce this result—and was that cost aligned with our values?

You need competence and execution; without them, "impact" is just wishful marketing. But if you only optimize for achievement, two things tend to happen: results improve for a while, and the human experience around you worsens. Here's what that can look like in practice: you hit the targets, but your team stops taking smart risks because everything gets punished; your best people become guarded and transactional because they don't feel seen; turnover rises; feedback dries up; meetings feel tense; at home you're physically present but mentally elsewhere. From the outside, it still looks like success. From the inside, the system is getting brittle. Impact brings the experience back into the frame.

C.A.S.T.
Curiosity – **Aim** - Send It – Tend It & Track

Three Channels of Impact

You are already having impact, whether you've chosen it or not. It tends to show up in three overlapping areas:

1. **People** – individuals and groups you touch directly.

2. **Systems** – organizations, processes, and cultures you shape.

3. **Places** – communities and environments you leave behind.

Let's move quickly through each.

1. Impact on People: The Wake You Leave Behind

Every leader leaves a wake, much like the disturbance behind a boat. Consider this: if five people who interact with you regularly were asked, "What's it like to be on the other side of them, day to day?" or "In three words, how does their presence land?", what would you hope they'd say, and what might they say?

Impact on people shows up in questions like: Do individuals grow or shrink around you? Do they become more capable and confident, or more dependent and cautious? Do they feel more honest and braver, or more guarded? Two leaders can both "get results," but one might leave a trail of exhausted high performers and thin relationships, while the other leaves people saying, "They made me better," or "This was some of the hardest work I've done, but I felt seen and supported." The pressure might be the same, but the relational impact is different.

<u>A Different Lens on Relationships</u>

In an interview with Sonja Lyubomirsky, the Dalai Lama offered two lines: - **"We are all each other's mothers"** – harming others is, ultimately, a way of harming ourselves. - **"Love is not a**

feeling, but a decision" – a series of choices about how we show up, not just a mood that comes and goes. For leaders, those ideas translate less into sentiment and more into practice: how you design your systems, how you give feedback, how you set boundaries, and how you decide whose interests you will and won't trade off under pressure.

Quick reflection – your relational wake

Pick three names at work and three at home. For each person, answer quietly:

1. Over the last 12–18 months, what has my presence *actually* done to them—emotionally, professionally, relationally?

2. If I could influence one thing about their life or growth in the next year, what would it be?

You're not writing an essay. You're reading the water.

2. Impact on Systems: The Cultures and Structures You Leave

Beyond individuals, you are always building or shaping systems: teams, companies, boards, partnerships, even extended families. You influence what gets rewarded, what gets tolerated, what quietly gets punished, and what never gets talked about.

Two leaders can inherit the same team and leave very different signatures. One drives short-term performance and leaves behind fear, politics, and narrow, short-term thinking. The other also sets a high bar, but leaves behind clarity, trust, and shared ownership that continue to pay dividends long after they've moved on. System-level impact shows up in whether values are visible in real decisions, or only on posters. "If I left tomorrow, what habits and norms would continue because of what I've modeled and reinforced?"

Over time, the way you lead becomes the way things are done around here. That is system impact.

Quick reflection – your system signature
Pick one system you meaningfully influence (a team, division, board, family business). Ask yourself:

- "If someone else stepped into this system after me, what would they notice I'd left behind?"
- "Where does this system reflect my stated values?"

The gap between "what I say I value" and "what my system rewards" is where your next round of work likely lives.

3. Impact on Places: The River Beyond You

Your impact isn't limited to people and organizations. It also touches places—the physical and social environments you move through. It shows up in the towns and neighborhoods your decisions touch. It reaches the rivers, trails, and landscapes you say you love. It shapes, in small and real ways, the local schools, clinics, nonprofits, and civic institutions that hold a community together.

You can't participate in an economy or a community without leaving marks. The question isn't whether you leave a mark, but whether your presence looks more like care and stewardship—or more like extraction and neglect. And this doesn't have to be abstract. It gets practical quickly: how does our business use or protect local resources? How do my own consumption and travel habits square with what I say matters? What modest, realistic version of "stewardship" fits this season of my life?

C.A.S.T.
Curiosity - **Aim** - Send It - Tend It & Track

You don't need a grand global cause for any of this to matter. The river you fish, the town your company operates in, and the school your kids attend are all part of your impact story.

Quick Reflection: The Places You Touch

Think of one place that matters to you—a river, a town, a neighborhood, a school. Consider how you or your organization's presence affected that place. If the place could talk about my impact, what might it say? Again, you're not writing a report. You're learning to see the broader river you're fishing in.

A Simple Impact Map: Your Current Portfolio

Impact is usually framed as outward—what you do to and for others. But every meaningful commitment also leaves a mark on you: your body, your nervous system, your integrity, and your relationships. So instead of evaluating commitments one at a time in isolation, it helps to see your whole portfolio at once.

Imagine a simple 2×2 map for your major commitments—work domains, core relationships, and key community roles. On one axis is your impact on others: what this commitment has actually changed for people, systems, or places (not your intentions, but real outcomes). On the other axis is the net impact on you: what it's doing to your health, your relationships, your capacity, and your ability to feel clean inside your own skin. When you hold both dimensions at the same time, most commitments fall into four recognizable categories.

Some **are high impact on others and a net positive for you**. These are your sweet spots—the roles where you're truly helping, and the work feels sustainable or even energizing. Over time, you want more of this category in your life, not because it's easy, but because it's aligned and it lasts.

C.A.S.T.
Curiosity – **Aim** - Send It – Tend It & Track

Some are **high impact on others and a net negative for you**. **These are heroic load zones**—work that clearly matters but is costs you more than it should. This is where good people quietly burn out, especially when the mission becomes an excuse to ignore the cost. These commitments may not need to be abandoned, but they need something: redesign, support, or a time boundary so "temporarily brutal" doesn't become your baseline.

Some are **low or unclear impact on others but a net positive for you**. These are the "good for me, unclear for them" roles—often hobbies, comforts, or legacy commitments you genuinely enjoy. You probably need some of this in a full life; the only question is how much of your time it's taking, and whether it's crowding out roles where your contribution is clearer.

And then there are the **low or unclear impact on others and net negative for you** commitments—the "why am I doing this?" zones. Dead meetings, stale roles, habits that serve no one. This is prime territory for change experiments, because even small cuts or redesigns here can free up disproportionate energy.

Impact on Self ↑	**Self Interest** Positive for me Negative/unclear for others	**Sweet Spot** Positive for others Positive for me
	Why do these? Negative for others Negative for me	**Heroic Zone** Positive for others Negative/unclear for me

Impact on Others ⟶

You don't need a spreadsheet. Just write-down or mentally place each major commitment into one of these buckets. The goal isn't precision—it's clarity. It's seeing your portfolio of impact, including the real costs, instead of living inside a blur of obligations.

Quick Reflection: One Small Rebalance

Looking at those four buckets, think about one single commitment, if shifted even slightly—exited, redesigned, or time-bounded—would free up meaningful capacity for higher-quality impact. That's the kind of question that quietly reshapes a life.

C.A.S.T.
Curiosity – **Aim** - Send It – Tend It & Track

From Vague Legacy to a Working Impact Statement

"Legacy" language gets fuzzy fast. We say things like, "I want to make a difference." Those instincts matter, but they're usually too vague to steer by.

It's often more useful to write a short, present-tense impact statement for this season—something specific enough that you could compare it to your calendar. For example: *In this season, I want my presence to grow three to five leaders who are more capable and more ethical than me, and to make my home feel like a place of safety and laughter for my family and our close friends.*

Or: *In this season, I want my presence to reduce confusion and anxiety on my team by bringing clarity and calm. I want to show my kids what it looks like to work hard without making work my whole identity. And I want to support one or two local organizations that are quietly doing unglamorous, essential work.*

No slogan exercise. No five-year plan. Just a few sentences that describe the kind of wake you want to leave right now.

Exercise: Your Draft Impact Statement

Take five minutes and jot down answers to two questions:

1. In this season of my life, **who or what** do I most want my life to positively impact?

2. If someone close to me wrote three sentences about my impact **five years from now**, what would I hope they'd say?

Then, turn your notes into a 2–4 sentence, present-tense impact statement. Call it "Draft 1." Let it be imperfect. You can refine it as you live with it.

Common Distortions to Watch For

As you sharpen your aim, a few predictable distortions show up.

One is the scaling reflex: *"If it doesn't scale, it doesn't matter."* You've been trained to think in Total Addressable Market (TAM) size and user counts. And yes—scale matters. But depth does too. A single direct report, a single teenager, a single stretch of river may feel your impact more deeply than any metric ever will.

Another is the martyr script: *"Impact justifies any cost."* It sounds noble—"Yes, I'm exhausted but this is too important not to carry." To be fair, short, intense seasons of sacrifice happen. The problem is when sacrifice becomes both identity and excuse, and the cost stops being temporary and becomes normal.

A third is equating impact with visibility—**confusing titles and spotlight with contribution.** Impact may even deepen as visibility shrinks. Second-row roles, quiet mentoring, and local work can matter more than one more big stage.

Impact as a Daily Question

"Impact" is easy to talk about at retreats. It only starts to change your life when it shows up in daily questions. Before a meeting, you quietly ask yourself, "Have I created conditions where everyone in the room feels safe offering a dissenting view?" Inclusive cultures don't just feel better; they make better decisions. Before a hard conversation, you wonder, "What do I want the impact of this to be on our relationship three months from now?" Once a week, look back at your calendar and ask, "Did last week look like the life of someone aiming for the impact?" This is where Aim meets Send It. You're no longer just asking, "What do I want to catch?" You're asking, "What do I want these casts to do?"

C.A.S.T.
Curiosity – **Aim** - Send It – Tend It & Track

Bringing It Back to the River

On a real river, the impact of forces at play is often quiet and cumulative. Consider a log, dislodged years ago, that still shapes the current. Even a simple footpath, worn by countless boots, dictates where people enter the water. These aren't dramatic, sudden events, but the result of repeated pressure applied in particular directions.

Your life works the same way. It happens through one-on-one conversations, through those unspoken "we don't talk about that here" moments, and every conscious or unconscious decision about where you choose to be present or absent. The truth is that you're already making an impact; the question isn't if you are, but what kind of impact it is.

For this chapter of your life, the central inquiry becomes: given the specific river you're in and the season you're experiencing, what kind of channels do you genuinely want your life to carve? It's an aspiration you won't get perfectly right—no one does.

Casting a tangled line just tightens knots. It's best to fix a line before you chase the fish. If you can assess your current impact, clearly articulate the impact you're aiming for, and then make small adjustments in that direction, you're Sight Casting your impact. You're not just throwing out a line and hoping for the best; you're intentionally shaping the wake you leave behind.

In the next chapter, you'll shift focus to identity: who you remain when roles change and how to stay anchored in your values and sense of impact through it.

Chapter 7 – Identity

"You may not control all the events that happen to you, but you can decide not to be reduced by them."

—*Maya Angelou*

This chapter speaks most directly to leaders navigating major transitions—role changes, kids launching, aging parents, and health shifts. If you're not in that season yet, treat this as a preview of the identity work that will matter later.

If values answer "What matters now?" and impact answers "What difference am I making?", then identity answers a quieter, more unnerving question:

Who am I when the roles and river change?

For much of your career, the answer may have felt simple. You're a CEO. A founder. You run the P&L. You're the one people call when things are on fire.

You may also carry equally weighty personal identities. Oldest child. Provider. Fixer. The one who keeps it together.

These identities are not trivial. They helped you do hard things and carry real responsibility. They can be a source of pride, energy, and meaning.

They also create a problem when life changes. Identity labels can shift when things change. Think about what happens when your role shifts or the company is sold. Or the board fires you. What occurs when a health issue prevents you from cycling and running, or when your children no longer require your support in the same manner? When change occurs, previous identity labels don't automatically update.

The river has changed. The roles on your calendar have changed. But inside, you may still be judging yourself by an old script.

This chapter is about bringing that script into view—understanding how your identity is built and how it can quietly become fused to specific roles and achievements. It explores what happens when the river of your life takes a sharp bend and how to relate to your identity in a way that is more spacious, grounded in your values, and less brittle. The goal isn't to eliminate your roles but to wear them more lightly, so you can remain true to yourself even as those roles evolve.

How Identity Gets Built (Often Without Your Consent)

Your identity is not the single thing you chose one afternoon. It's more like a braided current of early messages about who you had to be, roles you stepped into because someone needed you to, strengths that were praised (and weaknesses that were punished), and stories you've repeated about yourself—out loud and in your head—for years.

For high-responsibility leaders, certain stories show up again and again: "I'm the reliable one. I don't drop balls." "I'm the one who fixes things." "I'm the calm in the storm." "I am the primary provider. That's non-negotiable." These are not just passing thoughts; over time they become identity commitments. You organize your life to make them come true.

C.A.S.T.
Curiosity - **Aim** - Send It - Tend It & Track

So, you say yes more than is sane because "people count on me." You take the risky assignment because "I'm the one who can handle it." You avoid asking for help because "I'm supposed to be the helper." And because these identities have often led to real success, they don't initially look like a problem. They look like your edge.

Until the context changes.

When Roles Change Faster Than Identity

Earlier we looked at how life stages and shocks can reshape your values and circumstances. What often happens is that our **identity—our deep sense of who we are—lags these external changes.** Our inner story struggles to keep pace with the new reality.

You see this in familiar ways. The operator moves into a portfolio or advisory role but still measures their worth by how many operational fires they personally put out. The parents' kids leave home, but their inner world is still wired around being needed every day. A leader steps back from a 24/7 role for health or caregiving reasons yet continues to judge themselves by 24/7 standards. A founder sells the company but keeps introducing themselves—internally and externally—as though the sale never happened.

The recurring experience is similar: "I chose (or accepted) this change. On paper it's good. So why do I feel unmoored, smaller, or oddly invisible?" The answer is often that roles change faster than identity. The outer river bent. The inner story stayed straight.

If you don't work with that gap intentionally, two risks show up. One is clinging to old roles past their natural season. You keep over-operating, over-controlling, or over-giving because "this is who I am," even when it's harming you and others. The other collapses when a role is taken away. If one role was doing too much identity work—"CEO," "provider," "rock"—its loss can feel like the loss of self, not just the loss of a job or context.

Identity work is less about finding a new label and more about relocating your sense of self from "what I do" to "who I am when things change."

Field Story: Making the Sky Blue
A mentor of mine once gave me one of the cleanest examples I've ever heard of a portable, values-based identity—one that could survive role changes without losing its meaning.

When he was working at the EPA on the Clean Air Act, his six-year-old son asked what he did for work. He tried to explain it in adult terms—policy, regulation, the slow grind of protecting air quality. His son listened, thought for a moment, and then translated it into something truer and simpler: "Oh, Dad… you make the sky blue."

That phrase landed—not as a cute line, but as an identity. Not "I am an EPA official," or "I am a policy expert," but **I am a leader who keeps the sky blue.**

Years later, he moved on from the EPA and joined a trade organization focused on clean energy production. At a massive industry conference, he stood on a stage in front of thousands of people and told that same story. Then he connected the dots: in this industry, that's what we do—we keep the sky blue. Same aim, new river.

Eight years after that, as he was leaving that organization, a senior leader in the industry told him how much she still thought about that story—how much she loved it. Eight years later. A single sentence from a child had outlived job titles, org charts, and conference keynotes.

That's the power of an identity anchored in values and impact. It travels. It works at the EPA, it works in industry, and it still works after retirement—when you're doing nonprofit work, mentoring, or serving your community. The role changes. The river changes. But the aim holds: keep the sky blue.

Role, Self, and the "I Behind the Job"

It can help to distinguish three things that shape our experience. First, there are the **roles** we hold: CEO, board member, parent, caregiver, coach, volunteer. These are the positions we occupy in life. Second, there are the **stories** we attach to those roles—the interpretations and beliefs that often become deeply ingrained: "Real leaders never show weakness." "Good parents always show up." "If I'm not central, I'm irrelevant."

The third, which Acceptance and Commitment Therapy (ACT) emphasizes and is discussed more later, is **self-as-context**—the "I" that notices all of this. This is the part of you that is aware of thoughts, roles, worries, and hopes, but is not identical to any of them. Instead of defining yourself as your job, your feelings, or your history, ACT invites you to see yourself as the place where all of that is happening. Roles come and go, stories change with new evidence, and feelings surge and recede. But there is a continuous "you" that can notice all of that and still choose how to live.

In plain river language: the roles are like stretches of water that you float through—pools, riffles, rapids. The stories are your fishing tales about those stretches. The "you" behind it all is the angler who keeps floating downstream. When your identity is fused tightly to a single role or story, every change in the water feels like a threat to self. When you remember that you are the angler, roles and stories become important, but not ultimate. You can honor them without letting them define your entire existence.

Identity Fused to Achievement: "I Am What I Produce"

For many leaders, identity isn't just fused to roles—it's fused to output: **hitting the number, closing the deal, being the one who always delivers.** You get used to introductions that start with your title and your resume. And if you're honest, you may like it. It feels good to be known as the person who gets things done.

There's nothing inherently wrong with that—until achievement becomes the only safe identity you trust. Then rest starts to feel threatening: if I'm not producing, who am I? Delegation starts to feel threatening: if someone else can do it, what does that say about me? Even saying no can feel threatening: if I stop carrying everything, will I stop being valuable?

This **"I am what I produce"** identity has predictable costs. At work, you become the bottleneck, you over-function for your team, and you quietly stunt other people's development. At home, you struggle to be fully present when there's nothing to fix or close. Inside, you never feel fully "enough," because every achievement quickly becomes the new baseline.

From a Sight Cast perspective, identity fused to achievement is like only feeling like an angler when you're netting fish. You miss the craft of the cast, the beauty of the water, the people you're with—everything that gives the day its actual depth.

A Personal Note: When My Own Identity Was Too Narrow

For much of my career, I drew a lot of my identity from being the one who could "handle it." Take the messy role—John can handle it. Step into the turnaround—John can handle it. Manage the tough stakeholder—John can handle it. There was pride in that. There was also exhaustion.

When I began spending more time caring for an aging parent, my calendar didn't ask whether I could handle it. It just started filling with hospital visits, care decisions, logistics, and emotional load. I couldn't hold the same definition of "good leader" and "good son" and "good partner" without something breaking. My old identity—"the one who carries everything"—was suddenly not just unsustainable; it was mathematically impossible.

For a while, I just tried harder. I stretched my days, slept less, and clipped time with friends and my own recreation first. It felt temporarily heroic, and then it felt like failure.

Only when I consciously widened my sense of identity—from "the one who can handle it" to "the one who makes honest, values-based tradeoffs and lets some things be imperfect"—did the season become survivable. Nothing outside changed overnight. But the way I **saw** myself in that season changed. That was the opening.

Identity and Values: "Who Am I, Even If…?"

Values and identity are tightly linked. **Values ask, "What kind of person do I want to be?" Identity often answers, "I am the kind of person who…"**

The trouble comes when the "I am…" gets attached primarily to roles and outcomes rather than to values and qualities of action.

C.A.S.T.
Curiosity – **Aim** - Send It – Tend It & Track

Compare these two identity statements: "I am a CEO," versus, "I am someone who leads with stewardship and courage, wherever I am planted." Or, "I am the provider for my family," versus, "I am someone who takes responsibility for the people I love, including myself."

The first versions are fragile. If the role changes, the identity collapses. The second versions are portable. You can carry them into very different circumstances. If you step off the CEO track and onto a board, you can still lead with stewardship and courage. If income sources change, you can still take responsibility for the people you love—including making decisions together.

A practical way to work with identity is to rewrite some of your core "I am…" statements in values-based language, so they can travel with you as roles and rivers change.

Exercise: Drafting Portable Identities

Take a few minutes and write down 3–5 "I am…" sentences you suspect are running your life right now. Common examples are: "I am the one people can count on," "I am the fixer," "I am the high performer," or "I am the glue in this family."

Then, for each one, ask two questions:

What value is underneath this identity—responsibility, care, excellence, stability, courage, or something else?

And how could I rewrite this identity in a more values-based, portable way?

For example, you might go from "I am the fixer" to: "I am someone who brings calm, clear thinking to hard situations—and I don't have to fix everything alone." Or from "I am the high performer" to: "I am someone who brings care and excellence to what I commit to, in ways that are sustainable."

Notice what the rewrites do. They keep the best of the old identity—care, excellence, stability—while loosening the rigid, unsustainable parts like "always," "everything," and "everyone." You're not discarding who you are; you're **updating the story so it can survive the next chapters of your life.**

Identity in Transition: Grieving and Rewriting

We don't talk enough about grief in leadership transitions and life changes. Leaving a role you loved. Letting go of being "indispensable" at work. Accepting that your body will not let you work or recreate the way you did at 35. Realizing that your kids don't need you to be the daily problem-solver anymore. These are not just calendar shifts; they are identity losses.

If you skip the grief and rush to "What's next?" you often carry a low-grade resentment or sadness into the new chapter. Part of you is still looking back at the old stretch of river, missing who you were there. Allowing some grief—naming what you're losing, and what you're afraid you'll never feel again—is not self-indulgent. It's part of clearing space for a new, more honest identity to emerge.

A few questions can help you do that work: What am I afraid I'm losing about myself in this transition? What did this role or season allow me to feel about who I am? Which parts of that are truly gone, and which parts might be expressible in new ways?

You may discover that the thrill of building from scratch can show up in mentoring a founder or helping a child launch. The satisfaction of being relied on can emerge in community organizations or extended family, in healthier doses. The joy of

C.A.S.T.
Curiosity – **Aim** - Send It – Tend It & Track

mastery can appear in entirely new crafts—writing, teaching, or learning a physical skill—if you're willing to be a beginner again.

The point is not to replace one identity badge with another, but to stay in honest conversation with who you are becoming instead of clinging to who you used to be.

ACT and Identity: You Are Not Your Thoughts About Yourself

Acceptance and Commitment Therapy (ACT) offers two especially useful moves for identity work:

Defusion – noticing thoughts as thoughts, not truths.

Self-as-context – remembering that you are the space in which thoughts and roles arise, not any single one of them.

Applied to identity, this might sound like: "I'm having the thought that I'm only valuable when I'm producing." Or, "I'm noticing a story that if I'm not in charge, I don't matter." Or, "I see that the 'I must handle everything' story is loud right now." You don't argue with the thought or try to prove it wrong in the moment. You simply name it as a story and then ask: "If I set this story to the side for just a moment, what would my values ask me to do right now?"

Over time, this move creates a tiny but powerful wedge between "who I am" and "what my frightened or driven brain is saying about me." You don't stop having identity stories. You stop letting them run you without question.

A Few Identity Questions Worth Returning To

Identity work is not a one-time exercise. It's more like a recurring review, the way you'd re-evaluate a strategy or portfolio. Questions to revisit in different seasons:

- Who am I, besides my current role?
- What identities served me well in earlier chapters that are now quietly harming me or others?
- If someone I love described who I am, without mentioning any titles, what would I hope they'd say?
- Where is my sense of self overly fused to a particular role, achievement, relationship, or ability?
- What portable, values-based "I am..." statements do I want to live from in this season?

From a Sight Casting perspective, this is the identity question beneath all the techniques: "When the river changes, who do I remain?" Not "what title do I hold," not "how many fish did I land," but rather the kind of angler you are and how you move through the water—how you treat the people in the boat and respond when the conditions shift in ways you never would have chosen.

Pulling It Together: Identity as a Companion, Not a Cage

Identity will always be part of how you move through the world. You will always have roles and carry stories about who you are, just as others will have their own stories about you. The goal is not to become a blank slate. It is to build an identity rooted in values rather than roles—one that can adapt as the river changes and supports your happiness instead of sabotaging it.

When you see how your current identity was built, loosen its grip where it has become too tight, rewrite key "I am" statements in values-based language, and notice identity stories as stories—not commands—you create just enough space to choose which roles to hold onto, which to let evolve or go, and how to carry yourself when titles and circumstances inevitably change.

In the chapters that follow, as we get more practical about steps to take (Send It) and tracking, remember that you are not just optimizing a calendar or a set of goals. You are shaping the kind of person you are becoming—and the kind of angler you will be in the next bend of the river. That identity work is not separate from your leadership; it is the substrate underneath it.

Key Takeaways from Part II: Aim

In Part II, you moved from noticing the river to choosing your direction in it. You explored what matters now, difference you want to make, and who you remain when seasons change so your aim is true. The three core insights are:

1. **Values are an internal compass, not branding exercise:** You identified core values. Instead of chasing the next milestone, you can now rely on values to aim energy with intention, even as the river shifts, so you stop **under-aiming your own life** and over-aiming the business.

2. **Impact is about your wake, not just your wins:** You looked beyond achievement to the real footprint of your life: what your presence does to people, systems, and places. By mapping your "impact portfolio," you identified where your contribution is sustainable and where it is costing you too much, allowing you to draft a present-tense statement for the wake you want to leave.

3. **Identity travels when anchored in values, not titles:** You examined the stories you tell yourself—like "I'm the fixer" or "I'm the rock"—and how they fuse to specific roles. By rewriting these into portable, values-based language, you ensure your sense of self remains intact even when roles change, kids launch, or companies are sold.

Looking Ahead: From Aim to Send It

With a clear sense of what matters and the kind of angler you want to be, we will now turn Aim into action—designing experiments and building practices so your calendar and leadership reflect the values and impact you've named.

C.A.S.T.
Curiosity – **Aim** - Send It – Tend It & Track

PART III: SEND IT

Taking Action and Building Practices

Seeing clearly and aiming means nothing if you don't step forward and make the cast. Part III is where intention becomes action, where understanding transforms into practice.

Here you'll find practical tools you can use to build a life of fulfillment—from structuring your days, to working skillfully with your mind, to designing for peak experiences and deep engagement.

This is the **Send It** technique of the cast itself—the practices, skills, and habits that turn your values and aims into lived reality.

C.A.S.T.
Curiosity – Aim - **Send It** - Tend It & Track

Chapter 8 – Send It: Making the First Cast Count

"Often we are more frightened than hurt, and we suffer more from imagination than from reality."

—*Marcus Aurelius*

You've waded into the river, named values, and identified impact. Now we reach a moment of truth: the cast. **Send It** is how you act when something real is on the line. It's how you open a hard conversation, step into new roles, or frame recommendations.

Big Fish, One Shot

On the river, big fish are big for a reason. They've seen bad presentations before. They've watched flies slap the water and wading boots splash too close to their lie. When you're sight casting to a fish like that, you might only get one clean shot before it's spooked and gone.

In leadership, as on the river, it is almost always better to make one thoughtful, well-positioned cast than three sloppy, reactive ones. You may get another conversation, but you rarely get another true first impression. Rushing that first cast when it matters most can cost you chances you can't easily get back. In this book, Send It is that moment of first presentation—when something important is in front of you and you must make the cast.

C.A.S.T.
Curiosity - Aim - **Send It**- Tend It & Track

Why We Rush (or Freeze) When It Matters

If first presentations matter so much, why don't we make them more often? Most leaders I work with don't lack information; they lack space between seeing and doing. In that gap, the mind spins familiar stories—*Don't screw this up. You don't really know what you're doing*—while anxiety and urgency flood the system. This is the "suffering from imagination" Marcus Aurelius warned about: we lose our effectiveness not to the reality of the situation, but to the stories we tell ourselves about it.

Three patterns tend to show up. We **overthink**, staying on the bank replaying worst-case scenarios until we never cast. We **overreact**, getting hooked by urgency and throwing the line just to end the discomfort—sending the email too fast or making a hasty decision. Or we **over-rely on habit**, running the same old script of stepping in and carrying more, without asking whether that cast fits the water we're in now.

Send It isn't about perfection or over-engineering every move. It's about inserting just enough intention between *I see something* and *I do something* so your first presentation has a real chance of working—even when your inner weather is noisy. You're not going to feel calm and confident before every big moment. The real question is: *How do I make good, values-aligned casts with all that inner weather on board?*

A Tight Loop for Important Casts

When a conversation or decision counts, you don't need a twelve-step process. You need a loop you can run in thirty seconds:

Name the purpose: "What am I aiming at here—for me, for them, and for the system?"

C.A.S.T.
Curiosity - Aim - **Send It** - Tend It & Track

Next move: "What is the smartest, simplest next move that serves that aim?" (Not the whole strategy. Just the next cast.)

First presentation: "What would it look like to make that move cleanly the first time?" (Tone, timing, and medium.)

In the rest of this chapter, you'll ground that loop in two concrete areas where first presentations matter a great deal: how you enter and frame important conversations, and how you choose when to cast at all (and when to let the fish hold for now). Later, you'll add ACT skills that help you create this space on purpose—skills for stepping back from thoughts, making room for feelings, and coming back to this moment, this choice, this cast.

Entering Important Conversations: Position Before Presentation

On the river, where you stand matters as much as how you cast. If you throw your shadow over a fish, the quality of your loop won't save you. You already blew the approach.

Leaders do the same thing in conversations. They walk into a difficult 1:1 with no preparation or open with conclusions instead of curiosity. The other person is on the defensive before the conversation even starts. Send It starts before words leave your mouth. Before a meaningful interaction—especially about performance, conflict, or a significant change—run a quick internal checklist:

Impact: "What do I want the impact of this conversation to be two weeks from now—for them, me, the team?"

Values: "Which of my values do I want to embody here (e.g., honesty, stewardship, courage, care)?"

C.A.S.T.
Curiosity - Aim - **Send It-** Tend It & Track

Stance: "What role gives me the best chance—coach, partner, decider, listener?"

Assumptions: "How much do I know versus assume?"

Conditions: "Where and when should this happen for it to go well? Do we need privacy, enough time, or a neutral location?"

That's the leadership equivalent of pausing to watch how the fish is holding and then choosing your distance before you unspool line. You're not scripting the whole interaction. You're refusing to blind cast into a sensitive situation. (If you've read *Crucial Conversations* by Patterson et al., 2012, this checklist will be familiar—I'm offering a compact, river-based version you can run in 30 seconds.)

Field prompt

Think of a hard conversation you've been postponing. If you applied the prior section checklist, what would you change about *when* you have it, *where* you have it, and *how* you begin? Write down the first two or three moves you could make differently.

Making the First Presentation Count

A clean first presentation usually follows a few rules.

Name your intent early. People relax—or at least brace more productively—when they know why you're there: "I'm sitting down because I care about our working relationship and noticed some tension I don't fully understand."

Lead with data, not verdicts. Start with observable facts and how you're making sense of them, then invite their view: "I've noticed two deadlines slip this month. What's going on?"

Say the hard thing cleanly, once. Don't dance around the core message or hammer it repeatedly. State the non-negotiable plainly, hold steady, and leave room for the other person to respond.

Size the cast to the moment. Not every fish needs a long 60-foot cast. Not every issue needs a 90-minute summit. Send It also means right-sizing your action—nudge versus reset conversation, draft versus fully baked recommendation, single announcement versus a few touchpoints. Match the cast to the conditions: enough energy to get there, not so much that you blow the pool.

Choosing When *Not* to Cast

Sometimes the smartest move on the river is to wait. The fish are there, but they're tight to cover and you're more likely to lay a line across their fin than out in front of them where the fly belongs. Leaders often forget that restraint is part of Send It. Because you are conscientious and accountable, you may feel an urge to reply immediately to every difficult email or weigh in on every thread. Sometimes that's integrity. Sometimes it's anxiety.

Part of Send It is learning to ask: "Is this my cast to make?" "Would a pause to let emotions settle lead to a better presentation?" "Is not responding right now the wiser move?" One simple practice is to **wait overnight** before replying to a heated message, so you can respond from your values instead of from adrenaline (cf. David, 2016, on emotional agility and "showing up" rather than reacting). Or, hold back in a meeting to let a more junior leader step in with their view, even if your answer is already clear in your head. Jumping on everything that moves often creates more noise than progress. Intention sometimes looks like saying, "Not this one. Not yet. Not me."

C.A.S.T.
Curiosity - Aim - **Send It** - Tend It & Track

When You Won't Get It Perfect (and That's Okay)

Even with the best setup and the best first presentation, sometimes the fish just doesn't eat. You'll misread the current, misjudge the emotion, or say something far less artfully than you intended.

Send It with intention is not a guarantee of control—it's a way of increasing the odds that your actions align with your values and your aim. When a cast doesn't land, you have a choice: beat yourself up or get curious. Ask what you missed about the person, the context, or yourself. Ask what you learned that changes the next move. Ask what your values would have you do now—repair or adjust course. You aren't trying to become the leader who always says the right thing. You're becoming the leader who acts on purpose rather than by reflex, treating important moments like they're worth one thoughtful cast—and the learning that follows.

Exercise: A Simple Send It Scan for Your Week

Once a week, take ten minutes to list your "big fish" (one hard conversation, one key decision, and one commitment). For each, clarify your **Purpose**, **Next Move**, and **First Presentation**. Schedule the cast. This small scan changes the texture of your weeks. You treat high-impact moments with care and build a habit of learning from action instead of from rumination alone.

Where We're Heading Next

This chapter has been about making fewer, better casts and letting your first presentation reflect your values and aim rather than your anxiety. In the next chapter, you'll use Acceptance and Commitment Training (ACT) as a practical way to work with thoughts and feelings to keep your footing once you're in the river.

C.A.S.T.
Curiosity - Aim - **Send It** - Tend It & Track

Chapter 9 – Working With the River: ACT for Hard Casts

"Between stimulus and response there is a space. In that space is our power to choose our response."

—Viktor Frankl

Life will not cooperate with your plans. Markets turn. Parents have strokes. Children struggle. Bodies change. Roles end. Expectations collide. Even on quiet days, your mind can be loud—replaying, predicting. You can't control all of that. You can influence some of it. You can always choose how you respond. This chapter is about a practical way of doing that in real time: **Acceptance and Commitment Training (ACT).**

ACT isn't about "thinking positive," eliminating difficult emotions, or forcing yourself to be calm. It's about making room for the full range of your inner experience, staying connected to values, and taking committed action in their direction—even when your thoughts and feelings are messy. ACT helps you keep casting when the water blows out. You don't need perfect conditions in your mind to make a good cast. You need enough skill to work with whatever is happening inside while you act on what matters. For many leaders, ACT is more usable in the hallway between meetings than a full Cognitive Behavioral Therapy (CBT) thought record. This chapter stays simple on purpose. My aim is to provide one or two moves you can remember and use on a hard day.

C.A.S.T.
Curiosity - Aim - **Send It**- Tend It & Track

What ACT Is (and How It Differs From CBT)

Both ACT and Cognitive Behavioral Therapy (CBT) start from the same observation: thoughts and beliefs powerfully influence how we feel and act. Where they diverge is in what they ask you to do with those thoughts.

CBT says, in essence: "**Let's examine this thought.** Is it accurate? Is it distorted? Can we replace it with a more realistic, helpful one?" The focus is on changing the content of thinking.

ACT says: "**Thoughts are just thoughts**—passing events in the mind. We don't always need to replace them. Let's change your relationship to them so they don't run the show." The focus is on **changing your stance toward thoughts and feelings** and using **values as the compass for action.**

Each approach is well supported by research. You don't need to choose a side. Many therapists and coaches draw from both. For leaders carrying a lot of responsibility, ACT is often especially practical because you rarely have time in the moment to do a detailed thought record. You can't wait until you feel confident, calm, or positive before acting. You need something you can use between back-to-back meetings, on the phone with a doctor, or in the hallway before a tough conversation.

ACT gives you exactly that: a **few simple inner moves you can make while you're still in the river.**

Two Big Shifts

ACT rests on two core shifts in how you relate to your inner world. The first is recognizing that **thoughts and feelings are experiences, not commands.** Your mind produces a constant stream of commentary: "You're blowing this." "They don't respect

C.A.S.T.
Curiosity - Aim - **Send It** - Tend It & Track

you." "If you say no, you'll regret it." "You're failing everyone." Those sound like facts. They feel like orders. ACT invites you to treat them instead as events you're noticing—like headlines running on a ticker at the bottom of the screen, or leaves moving past you on the current. You don't have to argue with every thought. You also don't have to obey them.

The second shift is understanding that **values, not moods, decide your next move.** You can't always choose what you feel. You can always choose how you behave in the presence of that feeling. If this sounds familiar, it should—Stoic philosophers like Epictetus and Marcus Aurelius taught the same principle: focus on what you can control (your choices, your character) and let go of what you can't (outcomes, others' reactions, your own emotions). Instead of, "I'll have the hard conversation when I feel ready, calm, or confident," ACT asks: "Given that I'm anxious and my mind is noisy, what would my values have me do next?" You still feel the anxiety. You just don't let it drive the boat. Everything in this chapter is an expression of those two shifts.

Recognize A Thought…As Only A Thought: "I'm Having the Thought That…"

When your mind says, "This will be a disaster," ACT's simplest move is to add five words: **"I'm having the thought that** this will be a disaster." When your mind says, "I'm a failure," you shift to: **"I'm having the thought that** I'm a failure right now."

It sounds almost too simple. But that small language change does three things: it reminds you this is a thought, not a fact; it creates a tiny bit of space between you and the thought; and it buys you a moment to decide whether you want to act on this or not. You can play with other variations, like "I notice a story that they don't respect me" or "My mind is predicting that this conversation will

C.A.S.T.
Curiosity - Aim - **Send It**- Tend It & Track

go badly." You're not telling yourself the thought is wrong. You're just stepping out of automatic fusion with it.

Here is a leadership example. You're about to give candid feedback to a high performer who is also volatile. Your mind offers a familiar trio: "You're terrible at these conversations." "If you're direct, they'll resent you forever." "Just soften it and move on." Instead of fighting those thoughts or believing them, you quietly note, "I'm having the thought that I'm terrible at this" and "I'm having the thought that they'll resent me forever if I'm honest." Then you ask a different question: If I listened to these thoughts, what would I do? If I listened to my values—integrity, respect, and stewardship—what would I do?

You haven't made the anxiety vanish. You've just made it one voice in the room, not the chair of the board. That's defusion in ACT terms. For our purposes: **name the thought as a thought.**

Here is some practical shorthand. Whenever you notice a harsh, absolute, or fear-driven thought, prefix it silently with "I'm having the thought that…" Do that three or four times in one day and you'll feel a real difference.

Acting on Incomplete Information: A Leadership Parallel

In leadership, you rarely have complete information before you act.

I've lived it myself. I've joined companies that looked strong from the outside—compelling missions, appealing brands, seemingly solid cultures. It was only after I arrived that serious compliance or legal issues came to light.

Sometimes, people inside the organization had known about those issues and hadn't disclosed them. That created a problem of integrity for me. If there was no real appetite for transparency or repair, I eventually chose to leave.

More often, the issues weren't intentionally hidden. They simply weren't fully understood until someone started looking closely. In those cases, I realized: this is, in part, why I'm here. My job was to help establish policies, procedures, governance, team, and culture the business needed to scale profitably and responsibly.

In those moments, the work was deceptively simple. Before reacting from anger or panic, I had to pause long enough to:

- Assume positive intent where I reasonably could, rather than defaulting to blame.

- Get as clear as possible about the actual facts.

- Decide whether my values and the organization's response aligned well enough.

If they did, the next step was to pull up my big-boy pants and strengthen the system. If they didn't, the values-consistent choice was eventually to depart from the organization.

From an ACT perspective, this is exactly the kind of situation where your mind offers an immediate, vivid story—"They lied"; "This place is broken"; "You're trapped now"—and your first job is not to obey that story, but to notice it. You register the thoughts and the surge of feeling, assume positive intent where possible, then gather real data and check the situation against your values before you decide what to do.

C.A.S.T.
Curiosity - Aim - **Send It** - Tend It & Track

One Move for Feelings: "Where Is It in My Body?"

The second move is for feelings—anxiety, anger, shame, or grief—the tight cocktail you likely know from late-night emails and early-morning calls. Most of us have two default responses to these difficult emotions: we either fight them by pushing them down and drowning them in work or distraction, or we obey them by snapping, shutting down, or avoiding the hard conversations.

ACT offers a third option: making just enough space for the feeling that you can still choose your behavior.

A simple way to start is to shift from the story in your head to the sensations in your body. Pause for a moment and ask, "Where is this showing up?" Maybe it's a tight chest, a lump in your throat, knots in your stomach, or change in my tone of voice. Put a simple label on it: "Here is anxiety." "Here is anger." "Here is shame." Then, breathe into that area a few times. You aren't trying to relax the feeling away; you are proving to yourself that you can feel this and still be here. This is not relaxation; it's exposure in micro-form. You are teaching your nervous system: "I can feel this and still act from my values." You're not saying, "This is fine." You're saying, "This is here, and I'm willing to feel some of it if that's the cost of doing what matters."

Over time, that willingness is what lets you sit with a parent in the hospital without numbing out. It's what helps you stay grounded in a layoff conversation instead of going robotic or avoidant. And it's what allows you to hear tough feedback without instantly reaching for a defense.

Here is practical shorthand for this approach: Locate the feeling in your body, label it ("Here is shame"), and take three to five slow breaths. Then ask: "Given this, what do my values ask of me?"

C.A.S.T.
Curiosity - Aim - **Send It** - Tend It & Track

Field Story: When the River Blows Out

Two trips drove this home for me.

On one, I was invited to fish the Smith River in Montana—a coveted float trip people apply for permits years in advance. I was joining American Rivers staff, plus a writer and photographer doing a story for *The New York Times* about the river and the pollution risks of a possible copper mine. On day two, massive rains hit. The river blew out and our chances of good fishing dropped to almost zero. Our only realistic shots were tiny feeder streams. The fishing, to be blunt, sucked.

On another trip, my wife and I booked a long-anticipated float on the Middle Fork of the Salmon River. Days before we launched, storms triggered landslides and turned the river into another washed-out mess. The guides did everything they could: hiking us to clearer feeder creeks, shifting schedules, and when the water wouldn't cooperate, leaning into hikes and campfire music.

In both cases, the external reality was simple: the river was not what we wanted. Lots of anticipation met a blown-out torrent. The internal choices were less simple. We could lock onto the story—"This is ruined. What a waste."—or we could acknowledge the disappointment, feel it fully, and still choose what kind of days we were going to have. We did the latter, imperfectly. There were honest, grumpy moments. But they were more than offset by incredible views, great guides and their stories, and the rare chance to be off the grid—camaraderie, conversation, and perspective.

That's ACT in the wild: noticing the thought ("This trip is ruined") while making room for the feelings we earned by caring; and then asking, "Given all this, how can we still live our values today—adventure, connection, stewardship?" The water never got clear and the fishing never turned epic, but the trips were incredible.

C.A.S.T.
Curiosity - Aim - **Send It** - Tend It & Track

They became something else: practice in accepting what we couldn't change and re-aiming toward what still mattered.

Leaders don't get to pick their conditions either. Markets blow out. Health blows out. Team dynamics blow out. ACT is the skill of not letting the water conditions inside you ruin the entire trip.

Why This Matters for Leaders with Heavy Loads

You already know you will feel anxious, angry, sad, ashamed, and exhausted at times. You face situations that are unfair, painful, or unresolved for long stretches. You will rarely have the luxury of pausing your responsibilities until you feel better. ACT doesn't promise to remove that reality. It offers a different stance: less struggle with your inner life, more energy for what matters, and a clearer sense of yourself as one who can move in valued directions whether the internal water is calm or rough.

From a Sight Casting perspective, ACT is part of your **Send It** skillset. ACT helps you handle the cross-winds inside your own head and body so you can **still put the fly near your target**. In the Toolkit, you'll find a simple ACT Mini-Check you can run in 5–10 minutes when you feel stuck or flooded. It walks you through noticing thoughts and sensations, reconnecting to your values, and choosing one concrete next action. For now, it's enough to know that you don't have to fix your inner weather before you act; you just need a way to move with it. You'll build on this in the next chapters as we move into more concrete Send It tools—like Leading with Recommendations. For now, if you remember nothing else, remember these two moves: **"I'm having the thought that…"** and **"Where is this in my body, and what action would align best with my values?"** You don't control the river. You do control the cast. Make it count.

C.A.S.T.
Curiosity - Aim - **Send It** - Tend It & Track

Chapter 10 – Leading with Recommendations

"The leader's real test is whether decisions improve when they are made without them."

—*Peter Drucker*

If you lead a team or organization, this chapter is essential infrastructure. **If you only adopt a couple of practices from this book for your team, make this one of them.**

If you're an individual contributor or advisor, the principles still apply—you can model this approach and influence culture from any seat.

In the last two chapters, we focused on Send It from two angles: the **outer work** of making fewer, better casts, and the **inner work** of noticing your thoughts and feelings and still acting from your values (ACT). This chapter is about using the way you respond to problems to **develop others**—and to manage sideways and up more effectively.

One of the quiet killers of energy in organizations is the dynamic where everything "rolls uphill." A direct report brings you a problem, you ask a few questions, and before you know it, you're the one solving it. They walk out lighter. You walk out heavier.

This dynamic trains people to bring problems instead of solutions. It erodes accountability, weakens judgment, and keeps you in the center of every decision. The **Leading with Recommendations** model is a simple pattern that reverses this dynamic. It is a way to

C.A.S.T.
Curiosity - Aim - **Send It**- Tend It & Track

develop others while you run the business, by insisting that people come not just with issues, but with thinking.

That shift is not just about delegation. It's about teaching people how to think about problems in a structured way—so they become better stewards of the work, the team, and the organization's values. You're not just trying to get to the "right" answer. You're teaching people how to: think, own their work, and move from passive problem-spotting to active problem-solving. You're asking them to structure their thinking in four steps:

1. Situation assessment
2. Alternatives
3. Recommendation & Why
4. Next steps

This structure has roots in the disciplined decision-making cultures of companies like Procter & Gamble and Unilever. I learned early in my career at Unilever that clear recommendations beat vague problem statements. P&G's famous '1-pager' memo format trained generations of leaders to synthesize complex issues into situation, recommendation, rationale, and next steps—all on a single page. What I've adapted here takes that operational discipline and turns it into a developmental tool. Instead of a written memo designed primarily for upward communication, this is a conversational framework you can use to coach judgment, build ownership, and develop leaders at every level. The explicit focus on laying out alternatives prior to a recommendation with rationale makes this less about getting to 'yes' faster and more about teaching people how to think like owners.

When to Use the Leading with Recommendations Model

This model is a primary tool for managing direct reports and their teams. It is especially effective when they bring you unstructured problems rather than solutions, or when you find yourself re-deciding the same issues repeatedly. Use it when you want to raise the bar on ownership without micromanaging and to build a culture where people come prepared and think in tradeoffs.

It is less appropriate in a genuine crisis that requires immediate, directive leadership, or when there is a single, obvious course of action like legal or safety compliance. It is also not the place to start if someone truly lacks the context to begin; in those cases, model the thinking out loud first before asking them to take the lead. While this framework can influence bosses and peers, its primary aim is developmental: turning those without formal authority into leaders who think and act like owners. It's also valuable when you've become the bottleneck.

1. Assessment: "What's Really Going On?"

The first move is to require a concise articulation of the situation before anyone jumps to solutions. If a direct report brings you a problem like "we're having issues with the rollout," ask them to back up and provide background like this: "In terms of background, here's my understanding of the situation. We are committed to launch Feature X to our top 20 customers by March. Development is complete, but testing is behind by two weeks due to staff turnover. Two customers are already asking about delays, and sales is anxious about the impact on Q2 pipeline."

You are inviting them to do the work of synthesizing reality, not just forwarding you an issue from their messy inbox. You can

C.A.S.T.
Curiosity - Aim - **Send It** - Tend It & Track

coach toward this by asking for their one-paragraph summary of what's happening, the facts that matter, or the impact if you do nothing. Over time, people learn that showing up with a vague complaint isn't enough. The price of admission to your time is a thoughtful view of the situation, not just a forwarded headache.

2. Alternatives: "What Are Our Real Options?"

Next, your job is to train people to see choices, not just constraints. Many teams are conditioned to think there is only one possible path (often one they dislike), and they look to you to rescue them.

The **Leading with Recommendations** model asks people to lay out at least two or three plausible alternatives, each with real pros and cons. Instead of "We have a problem," you get something like: "I see several options. We can hold the original March 1 launch date, accept higher risk of bugs, and increase support staffing temporarily. We can delay the launch by two weeks, communicate proactively with our top 20 customers, and offer a small incentive for patience. Or we can do a phased launch with five to seven customers on March 1 and roll out to the rest two weeks later, using the early group to shake out issues."

Now you have something to work with. You're no longer staring at a generalized issue—you're working through tradeoffs. To reinforce the habit, I'll often set a simple expectation up front: before we meet, write down at least two alternatives you see (and one wild card if you've got it). Then we pressure-test the thinking: what's the best case and the worst-case for each option? If you had to explain these choices to the board in two minutes, how would you frame them? This step does two things at once. It raises the quality of decisions in the room, and it builds your people's ability to think strategically—not just execute tasks.

C.A.S.T.
Curiosity - Aim - **Send It** - Tend It & Track

3. Recommendation: "Given All That, What Do You Think We Should Do?"

This is the heart of the model. Many talented people stop short of making a call. They collect some data but slide the problem onto your desk like it's a hot pan they can't hold. When you ask for a recommendation, you tell them their job is not just to gather data but to take ownership. A good recommendation sounds like:

"My recommendation is to delay the launch by two weeks. It best protects long-term trust with our top 20 customers and reduces the risk of a messy launch that could damage our brand. We can mitigate revenue impact by continuing with our current product line until launch. The downside is short-term pressure on our Q2 pipeline, which I think we can manage by…"

You can coach this by asking what they would do if they had to decide right now, why they are recommending this path, and what they see as risks. Sometimes their recommendation will be spot on; sometimes it will be off. Either way, you have a view into their judgment, which is gold for development. You can affirm the thinking even if you adjust the decision by noting that you like how they weighed customer trust against the timeline, even if you ultimately lean toward a phased launch instead of a full delay. People stop waiting to see what "the boss thinks" and start building their decision-making muscles.

4. Next Steps: "Who Does What by When?"

Finally, you ask them to provide clear, time-bound next steps. Instead of ending with, "Okay, sounds good," the recommender follows with: "Based on the recommendation, here's are the next steps: I'll draft the communication plan by Friday and review it with you, Monday. I'll align with the team on the revised schedule

C.A.S.T.
Curiosity - Aim - **Send It** - Tend It & Track

this afternoon. I'll update sales leaders in next Tuesday's call." This is where accountability gets real. Ownership is not a feeling; it is commitments with names and dates. Reinforce this by making it a norm: before leaving a conversation, summarize the plan and who owns what, identify things that need to happen (and by when), and clarify how you'll know whether it worked. The model comes full circle: people share a structured view of the situation, a set of options, a recommendation, and a concrete path forward. Your role shifts from chief problem solver to coach and approver.

Using the Model as a Development Tool

The power of this model is not just in making better decisions—it's in how it changes the relationship between you and your team.

Each time someone uses this structure, you see where they're strong and where they struggle—framing well but avoiding a clear recommendation, for example. That gives you coaching opportunities to greater ownership. You'll notice patterns. One person may reliably underestimate risk. Someone else sees options but can't choose. Name these patterns explicitly as coaching, not criticism: "You frame situations really well. Where I want to push you is taking a stronger stand on your recommendation, especially when things are ambiguous." Over time, you're not just getting better proposals—you're growing leaders.

Watch for common traps. Don't use this as a gotcha. If someone comes unprepared, coach them through it before expecting the full structure. Resist immediately overriding a recommendation; even when you disagree, pause to understand reasoning first. Don't let "bring me a recommendation" become code for "figure it out alone"—you're still responsible for coaching, context, and final decisions. The goal is structured thinking, not abdication.

C.A.S.T.
Curiosity - Aim - **Send It** - Tend It & Track

Culture Shift: From "Bring Me Problems" to "Bring Me Recommendations"

If you commit to this model, it will eventually reshape the culture, as meetings will become more focused and shorter, people will prepare before taking your time, and the default shifts from escalating decisions to owning decisions, with appropriate checks.

You can make this explicit by explaining that, moving forward, when someone brings you an issue, you are going to ask them to structure it into four topics. Emphasize that the reason for doing this is not to make their life harder but that you want to support their growth and to make better decisions, faster. You don't have to roll this out with a lot of training. Start with a simple prompt the next time someone brings you a problem:

"Before I weigh in, walk me through it in four steps:

1. What's the situation as you see it?

2. What are the main options?

3. What do you recommend and why?

4. What are the next steps related to your recommendation?"

Although the model works well as a tool to develop direct reports, it also travels well upward and sideways. When you use it with your board or peers, you respect their time by bringing clarity. You show up as someone who owns their domain, not someone who just passes messages along.

The key is to remember the primary purpose: building a culture where people without formal authority still act like owners—they assess, they generate alternatives, they recommend, and they commit. The first few times, they may stumble. That's okay. You're not just trying to get an answer; you're building a muscle in them and in your culture. You'll find people start showing up already thinking this way. And that's when you know the model has done its deeper work: it hasn't just helped you make better decisions—it has raised the level of leadership across the system.

Field Story: What Would Yola Say?

During my time at Burt's Bees, I worked with Yola Carlough who was the Director of Sustainability. On the org chart, I was more senior. In practice, I felt like I reported to her. Yola was one of the most principled, wise, and enlightened leaders I've ever met. She would speak her mind—respectfully, with a special way of infusing humor that made hard truths easier to hear. When I was wrestling with a decision, she would help me brainstorm alternatives, and then she would tell me her recommendation. Not tentatively. Not waiting to see what I thought first. She would make a call, regardless of her formal authority. I learned quickly to consult Yola on certain topics and to keep her informed on others—not because the org chart required it, but because she had earned enormous credibility and influence. People listened to her. Even years after we stopped working together, I would still hear her voice when facing a tough decision: What would Yola have to say about this? The lesson: you don't need a title to lead with recommendations. Yola modeled what this chapter is about—showing up with clear thinking, structured alternatives, and the courage to make a call. That's what builds influence, trust, and lasting impact. Unfortunately, Yola passed away in 2025. I'm grateful I remained in touch with her and that I told her directly about the positive impact she had on me.

C.A.S.T.
Curiosity - Aim - **Send It** - Tend It & Track

Role Clarity: The Foundation of Effective and Fulfilling Leadership

One of the quietest thieves of both performance and fulfillment in almost every organization is chronic role confusion. When it's unclear who owns what, who decides, and what "a good job" looks like, people don't just become inefficient; they become anxious. They over- or under-function, second-guess themselves, duplicate effort, or wait for someone else to move first. The river may be full of opportunity, but no one is sure which stretch they're supposed to fish.

From a distance, role clarity can sound like bureaucracy—org charts, job descriptions, swim lanes. Up close, when done well, it's an act of care. It tells those you lead, "Here is what I'm counting on you for. Here is what you don't have to carry. Here's how we'll know together if you're succeeding." It also tells you, "Here's what I own this season, and what I don't."

Without that clarity, your own over-responsible patterns fill the vacuum. If you're wired to fix things, you'll wade into every pool, offering opinions on everything from pricing to product design, whether it's yours to decide or not. In the short-term, that can feel helpful. In the long-term, it erodes others' confidence, clogs decision-making, and leaves you depleted—especially if you're also asking people to "lead with a recommendation." The mixed signals are obvious.

Frameworks like RACI (Responsible, Accountable, Consulted, Informed) and DARCI (Driver, Approver, Responsible, Consulted, Informed) aren't magic and can be overused, but they provide a common language for ownership and decision rights. Applied thoughtfully to recurring decisions and major initiatives, they reduce the ambient ambiguity that quietly wears people down. They make it easier for someone to say, "On this, I am responsible," or just as importantly, "On this, I am not."

C.A.S.T.
Curiosity - Aim - **Send It**- Tend It & Track

The deeper move is treating role clarity as a living conversation, not a one-time document. As the river changes—new markets, reorganizations, personal shifts—roles need to shift. What was sustainable to hold two years ago may no longer be wise today. If you never revisit those agreements, everyone operates on outdated maps, and resentment grows in the gap between expectation and reality. During reorganizations or strategic planning retreats, it can be eye-opening to ask the team which areas feel least clear; leaders are often surprised by the level and impact of ambiguity.

Some of the most powerful leadership conversations are the simplest: "Let's talk about your role this year. Here's what I see as your core responsibilities. Here's where I may be unintentionally stepping in." Or, "Given everything, here's what I can realistically own this season, and what I need to hand off."

For high-responsibility leaders, role clarity is also self-protection. Naming what you will and won't own prevents your identity as "the one who can handle it" from expanding until it crowds out your health and relationships. It's stewardship not only of your organization but of your own finite attention and energy.

When clear roles combine with a recommendation-led culture, something important happens. People know what they own, so they can lead within that domain. They know when to bring you a decision and when to keep you informed. You, in turn, can trust that important decisions are made by those who understand their lane, reserving your full engagement for the stretches of river that truly require your presence. Role clarity isn't just operational hygiene; it directly shapes whether your leadership life feels like a sustainable, meaningful use of you—or an endless, amorphous effort to be everywhere and everything at once.

C.A.S.T.
Curiosity - Aim - **Send It** - Tend It & Track

Chapter 11 – Invest in High-Trust Relationships

"The power of the world always works in circles, and everything tries to be round."

—*Black Elk*

When most of us imagine a happy or fulfilling life, we don't picture a spreadsheet. We picture people.

The moments that stand out—holidays, big wins, quiet Tuesday nights—are almost always relational. That's not a coincidence. Long-running research on adult development, including the Harvard Study of Adult Development, points to a clear conclusion: the quality of our close relationships is one of the strongest predictors of our overall happiness and life satisfaction.

What's less obvious is that the same relational patterns that predict happiness also drive effectiveness. Teams and leaders who perform best over time tend to be the ones with high trust and psychological safety—the shared belief that the team is safe for interpersonal risk-taking (Edmondson, 2019)—honest and frequent feedback, and a felt sense of "we're in this together."

This chapter is about investing in relationships on purpose, as health and effectiveness are inextricably linked. Feeling connected and supported doesn't just make life more enjoyable; it makes you braver, more creative, and more resilient. Doing meaningful work with people you trust is one of our deepest sources of satisfaction.

C.A.S.T.
Curiosity - Aim - **Send It-** Tend It & Track

What High-Trust Relationships Look Like at Work

"High trust" can sound abstract, but in your day-to-day work, it's incredibly concrete. Over time, people experience high trust with you when they can count on at least five behaviors:

You do what you say you'll do. You follow through, or you renegotiate early when you can't.

You tell the truth. You don't hide bad news or sugarcoat to avoid discomfort.

You actually listen. People feel heard before you decide. You're willing to ask, "What am I missing?" and mean it.

You care about them as a person, not just a role. You know some of what's happening in their life. You show interest beyond the task list.

You are willing to repair when you screw up. You apologize without defensiveness and make a visible effort to do better.

Trust isn't built in one offsite or one dramatic conversation. It's built through small, repeated interactions that signal, "It's safe here. We can tell the truth, and we'll still be okay." To be more deliberate about those interactions, it helps to have a simple mental model for what makes someone feel 'safe' with you. One of my favorite ways to break this down is the Trust Equation.

A Simple Model: The Trust Equation

A mentor and fellow coach, Ben Sands, was the first person to introduce me to Charles Green's "Trust Equation," from the book *The Trusted Advisor* (by David Maister, Charles Green, and Robert Galford). They describe trustworthiness with a formula:

$$\text{Trustworthiness} = \frac{\text{Credibility} + \text{Reliability} + \text{Intimacy}}{\text{Self Orientation}}$$

The "equation" isn't math; it's a heuristic. You don't need to calculate it. You use it to ask, "Which part needs attention here?" In plain language:

Credibility – "Do I believe what you say?"
Your expertise, judgment, and how honestly you communicate.

Reliability – "Do you do what you say you'll do?"
Your follow-through, consistency, and timeliness.

Intimacy – "Do I feel safe telling you the truth?"
How comfortable people feel sharing concerns, fears, mistakes.

Self-orientation – "Who is this really about—me, or you?"
When your behavior is mostly about protecting, proving, or advancing yourself, self-orientation goes up—trust goes down.

Think about the people you trust most. They tend to:

- Know what they're talking about (**credibility**),
- Do what they say they will (**reliability**),
- Make it feel safe to be honest and imperfect (**intimacy**),
- And show in lots of small ways that they're oriented toward your success, not just their own (**self-orientation**).

In my experience, many leaders intuitively understand the credibility and reliability parts of the equation. They know they need to be competent and consistent. Some even recognize how important it is to keep their self-orientation in check.

Yet when trust breaks down on a team, it's rarely because people suddenly stopped being competent—it's usually because

C.A.S.T.
Curiosity - Aim - **Send It** - Tend It & Track

something in the relationship feels unsafe. Where many leaders struggle is the intimacy piece: being appropriately vulnerable and open so people feel safe being honest. By vulnerability, I don't mean oversharing—I mean naming what's real: uncertainty, limits, mistakes, or needs. Leaders often want trust while staying emotionally armored, but that's a hard combination to sustain. Why would someone tell me they're struggling if I never show that I need support sometimes, too?

Over the years, I've noticed the leaders who build the deepest trust are the ones who know what to do in those subtle, uncomfortable moments when someone shares something real. My friend and colleague Mo Fathelbab gave me language for this.

Field Story: The Vulnerability Ladder (Mo Fathelbab)
Working with Mo Fathelbab, a pioneer in building trust in forums, I learned the idea of a "vulnerability ladder." When someone shares something vulnerable, the next response matters. If others "ladder down"—meeting or deepening that level of vulnerability with their own honest sharing—trust increases. If they "ladder up"—lightening the mood, changing the subject, or responding with something much less vulnerable—the original speaker can feel exposed and shut down. As a leader, learning to stay present with someone else's vulnerability, and to respond with appropriately vulnerable honesty of your own, is one of the fastest ways to build real trust.

Same Needs, Different Paths: Why Trust Matters

This practice of staying present with vulnerability is so effective because it addresses what lies beneath the surface of our professional personas. Ben Sands often reinforces this point with leaders: at a basic level, we all share the same human needs. You can map those needs to Maslow's hierarchy—from safety and belonging to esteem and self-actualization.

Where we **start to diverge** is in the **values we organize around**, and the **behaviors we use to meet those needs**.

Two people might both care deeply about security, but one expresses it through risk-averse planning, and the other through aggressive growth. Both crave belonging, but one reaches for frequent check-ins, and the other prefers long blocks of solo work.

The needs are similar; the behaviors and values that sit on top of those needs can look different. That's where friction comes from.

Without trust, those differences surface as "he's controlling," "she's checked out," and/or "they don't care." With trust, those same differences can be understood as: "We're trying to meet the same needs in different ways. Let's talk about it."

Trust allows us to stay in conversation to see past stories and co-create ways of working that honor everyone's needs.

Trust as the Foundation of High-Performing Teams

Patrick Lencioni's work on *The Five Dysfunctions of a Team* gives us another helpful lens. In his model, trust sits at the very bottom of the pyramid as the foundation (Lencioni, 2002). **Without trust, the other levels of the pyramid—healthy conflict, genuine commitment, accountability, and an attention to collective results—simply cannot stand.**

When that foundation of trust is missing, the entire team dynamic shifts into a defensive crouch. Conflict becomes political or personal rather than productive. Commitment turns into surface-level compliance. Because no one owns the decisions, accountability is avoided. Ultimately, results become uneven and harder to sustain because the team's goals are secondary to individual agendas.

When trust is strong, however, those same dimensions become natural and fluid. People feel safe enough to disagree without it becoming destructive, which allows them to commit to decisions they didn't originally propose. They can hold each other to high standards without defensive drama because they know the intent behind the challenge is mutual success.

Lencioni's model and Green's Trust Equation are essentially looking at the same dynamic from two angles. While the equation describes what individual trustworthiness feels like, the pyramid describes what happens at the team level when that trustworthiness is present or absent.

One of the clearest signals of that foundation is what happens around feedback. If you want to know how much trust exists on your team, don't start with survey results—look at how people handle bad news, disagreement, and hard truths. In high-trust environments, people can surface bad news, disagree, and share hard truths without bracing for impact. In low-trust environments, those same conversations get avoided, sanitized, or weaponized. How you handle feedback, especially when it's uncomfortable, may be the single most visible test of trustworthiness as a leader.

In the next chapter, you will zoom in on feedback itself—how you ask for it, give it, and respond to it—in ways that reinforce, rather than erode, the trust you're trying to build.

Chapter 12 – How Feedback Fuels Trust and Impact

"How we spend our days is, of course, how we spend our lives."

—*Annie Dillard*

In this chapter, you'll explore how to treat feedback as ongoing relationship maintenance rather than a high-stakes performance event and how to use a simple loop you can remember in real time. You'll also look at how to build containers—from weekly 1:1s to structured group sessions—that make honest feedback safer, and how to receive feedback in a way that lowers defensiveness and deepens trust. You'll see that none of this is abstract; these are small, repeatable casts you can make every week.

Feedback as a Trust Practice, Not a Performance Event

In many organizations, feedback is treated like a scheduled medical procedure. It happens once or twice a year and it is administered formally. Everyone braces.

You may believe feedback is important, but if it only shows up in performance reviews or in conflict after something goes wrong, it will never feel normal or safe.

High-trust teams do something different. They treat feedback as **ongoing relationship maintenance**: small, frequent adjustments

C.A.S.T.
Curiosity - Aim - **Send It**- Tend It & Track

instead of rare, dramatic interventions. Feedback in that context isn't just about fixing problems. It's a way of saying: "I care enough about you—and what we're building together—to tell you the truth. And I care enough about my own growth to ask for the truth back."

Coaches often reinforce with clients that "feedback is a gift"—but it's only a gift if people feel relatively safe giving it, and they see you take it seriously and **do something with it**. That second part is crucial. When you ask for feedback and visibly act on it, you make it much easier for people to give you feedback in the future. You're modeling several things. You are showing that feedback is **information**, not a verdict. You view it as a **gift**, not an attack, and you show that their effort to tell you the truth was **worth it**.

Over time, credibility and reliability go up, intimacy goes up, self-orientation goes down, and the team's ability to engage in healthy conflict and accountability improves.

A Simple Feedback Loop: Ask → Mirror → Align → Commit → Follow Up

Here's a structure I use with leaders and teams. It's simple to remember and robust enough to transform relationships. You don't need a special meeting to use it; it fits naturally into weekly 1:1s, project debriefs, or even quick hallway conversations.

You start by **asking for feedback** and making that a normal part of how you work. You might ask, "What is one thing I should start doing to better support you?" "What is one thing I should stop doing that makes your work harder?" or "What is one thing I should continue doing because it really helps you?" When leaders ask questions like this regularly, they send a clear signal: feedback is not something I do to you, it's something we do together.

C.A.S.T.
Curiosity - Aim - **Send It** - Tend It & Track

From there, you **mirror back what you heard**. You might say, "Let me make sure I've got it. I'm hearing that when I jump in with my solution, it makes it harder for you to own the problem. Did I get that right?" Or, "It sounds like you're saying our weekly status meeting feels rushed and doesn't leave room for real discussion. What am I missing?" Mirroring slows you down so you don't jump straight into defending or explaining. Mirroring is especially important across difference—seniority, gender, race, or background. It checks whether your message is landing as intended and signals their perspective matters. It lets the other person clarify what they meant. It shows that you value their perception as real data, not something to swat away. Especially when feedback is about a behavior they observed, their perception is their reality. You don't have to agree with every interpretation, but you do want to understand what they experienced.

Next, **align on what matters most**. Not everything in a feedback conversation is equally important or equally actionable. After mirroring, you zoom in together: "Of everything you shared, the part that feels most important for me to work on is…" or "If I only changed one thing here, what would make the biggest difference?" You're not grading their feedback; you're choosing where to start.

Then you **commit to a specific next step**. This is where good intentions often die. Leaders say, "Thank you, that's helpful," and nothing visible changes. Instead, make a clear, behavioral commitment: "Between now and our next 1:1, I'm going to make sure everyone on the team speaks once before I offer my view." Or, "For the next two client calls, I'll ask for your proposed solution before I share mine." Or, "In our next three 1:1s, I'll reserve at least five minutes at the end to ask you what's working and what's not." Specific, time-bound commitments build

C.A.S.T.
Curiosity - Aim - **Send It**- Tend It & Track

reliability. People start to believe you when you say, "I want to get better."

Finally, you **follow up in a future session**. This is the step that turns feedback from a one-time conversation into a trust-building engine. In your next 1:1 or check-in, you circle back: "You shared that our status meetings weren't working. I changed the agenda and left ten minutes for open discussion. Did that help? What should we tweak next?" When you do this consistently, people learn: "If I take the risk to give this person feedback, they will do something with it—and then they'll come back and ask what I'm seeing now." That pattern—especially the follow-through—is what makes it easier and easier for people to bring you honest input in the future.

Field Story: Group Feedback Sessions

One of the most powerful tools I've experienced and helped implement is a structured feedback session where **1:1 feedback is given in front of your whole team**.

This radical approach is designed to establish and leverage trust while normalizing feedback. The concept is as follows. Periodically, a leadership team participates in full-day sessions where each person, one by one, sit in the "hot seat," and the rest of the team shares feedback with them in real time. The feedback relates to just a couple of areas, typically framed as something like this:

- Here are 2-3 things I love and appreciate about you and your work

- Here are 2-3 areas where I think you could be more effective

When I was first introduced to this approach, the sessions were facilitated by a third-party expert, which mattered. Having a skilled, neutral facilitator created structure, set norms, and helped the group navigate the emotions that inevitably come with that level of candor.

Personally, I always felt a knot of anxiety leading up to those sessions. It's vulnerable to sit there, in front of people you work with every day, and hear their unfiltered perceptions. But almost every time, I walked away from those sessions feeling extremely grateful for the courage it took my colleagues to be that honest and for naming patterns so I could see them clearly as common themes. I was also grateful to be able to give feedback in a safe environment and be thanked for doing so.

As a coach, I now propose and facilitate similar group feedback sessions with clients—usually as part of their annual retreat or periodic strategic planning meetings. These sessions are **not** something you drop in casually. They require time to build trust on the team before you ever put someone in the "hot seat." They also require clear expectations, guardrails, and a thoughtful facilitator who can hold the space while protecting psychological safety. Often, the first sessions are not about highly personalized, pointed feedback. Instead, they focus on sharing some vulnerabilities, exploring individual working styles, and naming overall team strengths and weaknesses.

This round helps the team get comfortable with the format and with talking honestly about the work and themselves without immediately diving into deep 1:1 critique. Over time, as trust and skill grow, these sessions become more personalized. Individuals begin to receive clearer feedback about their specific impact, and the group reflects themes they see across different contexts. Ultimately, people start to hear more than just one person's view;

C.A.S.T.
Curiosity - Aim - **Send It** - Tend It & Track

they hear a consistent pattern emerging from several voices, which turns the feedback into a shared mirror held up by the entire team.

Hearing feedback as themes from multiple teammates makes it feel less like one person's opinion and more like a shared **mirror** the group is holding up together. It's intense work. It's not for every team, and it's not where you start on day one. But for teams that have built enough trust and are ready for it, thoughtfully facilitated group feedback sessions can dramatically accelerate both trust and growth. And, when teams can give and receive direct feedback in front of each other, the private 1:1 loops get easier, not harder.

Re-Forming the Team When People Join or Leave

Even when a team has done the hard work to build trust, it's not a one-time achievement. Teams are living systems. Every time a key person joins or leaves, the rhythms, unspoken norms, and informal alliances all shift.

In those moments, you can either pretend nothing has changed and hope the old trust somehow stretches to fit—or you can deliberately **re-form the team**.

Field Story: "As of Today, We Are a New Team"

I would like to share a memorable moment when I joined an executive team at a well-known brand that was tremendously successful by every measure. At my first staff meeting, the CEO asked me to introduce myself. He then insisted that a long-tenured colleague re-introduce himself after I did. When my colleague said it wasn't necessary as we had already met several times, the CEO replied, "As of today, we are a new team, and I would like each member of the team to introduce themselves."

That simple act reframed the room. It underscored that whenever a team's composition shifts, the trust and identity of the group have to be **rebuilt—not assumed**. Feedback is part of that re-forming. When the team changes, you have a natural opening to reset expectations about how you'll give and receive feedback. You will invite new voices into the feedback loop and can ask, explicitly, "What do you need from me now that we're a new team?" Those conversations help the new team co-create new trust patterns instead of inheriting ones that no longer fit.

Weekly 1:1s as the Container for This Work

You don't need a big offsite to practice some elements of this framework. Weekly 1:1s are one of the most underused levers leaders have for happiness and performance. Most 1:1s drift toward status updates—what's on your plate, what's stuck, what's next. Useful, but incomplete.

If you want your relationships and people—to grow, 1:1s also need to be a place where you talk about how you're working together, not just what you're working on. This doesn't require a therapy session. It can be as simple as reserving a few minutes at the end to ask what's one thing you're doing that's helping and what's one thing you could do differently to support them better.

You can invite your direct reports to ask you for feedback, too. Tell them that every few weeks, you'd love them to ask what's one thing they can do to grow faster in the role and commit to always giving them something concrete. When feedback becomes a standing ingredient in your weekly 1:1s—and when people see you act on it—it stops feeling like a special event and starts feeling like part of how you do business together.

C.A.S.T.
Curiosity - Aim - **Send It** - Tend It & Track

Getting the Balance Right: Positive and Constructive Feedback

Normalizing feedback is about **frequency** and **balance**.

If most of the "feedback" people get from you is corrective or critical, they will eventually stop listening—or they will listen from a defensive crouch. This is especially true for those new to leadership or underrepresented at the table. Check: are you giving everyone specific, developmental feedback—or do some get coaching while others get praise?

Most of us need more positive than corrective input to stay open and motivated. Aim for at least a 3:1 balance over time—several genuine, specific, positive pieces of feedback for every one corrective one. Research on relationships and team dynamics suggests that positive-to-negative interaction ratios of 3:1 or higher are associated with better outcomes (Gottman, 1994). It also means **thinking about the overall pattern**, not forcing a "compliment sandwich" in every conversation.

Used well, positive feedback helps people see what's working so they can do more of it, while also building psychological safety and goodwill that allows hard truths to land.

Constructive feedback is still essential. The point isn't to avoid it. The point is to **stack the deck** so that when you offer a harder message, the other person has enough positive experience with you that they can actually hear it—and act on it.

A Simple Pattern for Giving Constructive Feedback

Normalizing feedback means getting comfortable with the "hard casts"—those moments where you have to address a behavior that isn't working. When you need to offer constructive feedback, a simple three-part pattern keeps the conversation grounded in facts rather than character attacks.

You start by **naming the behavior you observed**. Be as specific as possible and avoid questioning their intent. Instead of saying, "You were being dismissive in the meeting," try: "In the meeting this morning, I noticed you interrupted Sarah three times before she could finish her proposal." You are describing a video recording of the event, not your interpretation of their heart.

Next, you **name the impact**. Explain how that behavior landed on you, the team, or the project. You might say, "When those interruptions happened, the room went quiet, and I'm worried we missed the core of her recommendation. It also makes it harder for the rest of the team to feel safe sharing new ideas." This is where you share the data of the impact without making it a verdict on their personality.

Finally, you **state your needs and wants** by ending with a clear request for the future. For example: "Moving forward, I need you to let others finish their thoughts completely before you weigh in. If you disagree, I want you to reflect back what you heard them say first, then offer your counter-point."

By following this **Behavior → Impact → Needs** sequence, you aren't asking the other person to defend their soul; you're asking them to look at a specific action and its consequences. It makes the feedback actionable and keeps the relationship intact. As we discussed with the "Assume Positive Intent" move, you can even lead into this pattern with curiosity by asking what was happening from their side before you add in the impact and your needs. This keeps the cast accurate and more likely to land where intended.

C.A.S.T.
Curiosity - Aim - **Send It** - Tend It & Track

Receiving Feedback: Reflection Over Rebuttal

You can't control how others give you feedback. You can control how you listen, what you assume, and what you do with it. Most feedback breakdowns aren't a skill problem; they're a state problem—defensiveness. The 15 Commitments of Conscious Leadership opens with Responsibility and Curiosity: own your part first, then get genuinely curious about what you might be missing (Dethmer, Chapman, and Klemp, 2014).

Treat behavior-based feedback as real data. If someone is describing something they saw or heard—"In that meeting, when you did X, it landed like Y"—their experience is real. It might not match your intent, but it's valuable information about your impact. Separate intent from impact. You know what you meant to do. They know how it landed. Both matter. The feedback moment is usually not the place to persuade them your intent was pure. It's a time to understand their experience. Choose reflection over rebuttal. In my experience, trying to explain or defend yourself right away rarely helps. It shuts the other person down and makes it less likely they'll be honest again. A more useful pattern is to:

- Listen all the way through.
- Mirror back what you heard: "What I'm hearing is... Did I get that right?"
- Ask for one or two concrete examples if you need them.
- Thank them and then take time on your own to reflect.

If, after reflection, you still feel a disconnect, you can revisit it later—in a calm, productive way: "I've been thinking about the feedback you gave me. Here's what I took from it and am trying. There's a piece I'm still wrestling with—could we talk more about that?" That posture lowers self-orientation and increases intimacy. It's also what makes you much easier to work with.

C.A.S.T.
Curiosity - Aim - **Send It** - Tend It & Track

Assume Positive Intent (Without Being Naïve)

When you're giving or receiving feedback, your default stance toward the other person matters as much as your wording. A simple cast forward is to assume positive intent. That doesn't mean assuming the behavior was good. It means assuming the person is trying to do well, given what they see and feel.

When you don't do this, it shows up in small but costly ways. A manager criticizes a direct report for "missing a deadline," only to discover later that the report was in her spam box. The damage to trust is done. A colleague misses a meeting because of a family emergency, and our first move is to express disappointment about their "lack of commitment," instead of asking if they're okay.

In each case, there's a fork in the road. The low-assumption path leads to "They messed up. They don't care." The positive-intent path leads to "Something might be going on I don't see yet." Assuming positive intent nudges you toward the second path. Your nervous system softens. You're more likely to be curious than accusatory, which makes it safer for both of you to look honestly at what happened and what needs to change.

You can bake this into feedback with one simple move: start with curiosity, "Hey, I noticed X. Can you walk me through what happened from your side?", then add impact: "Here's how that landed on the team." You're not ignoring what happened. You're starting from "help me see what you saw," then naming the effect.

Assuming positive intent is a starting position, not a blindfold. It doesn't mean ignoring patterns of harmful behavior or handing out trust without boundaries. You can assume positive intent and still name impact clearly or change the roles or decision rights.

C.A.S.T.
Curiosity - Aim - **Send It** - Tend It & Track

Relationships as Multipliers of Happiness and Effectiveness

If the other levers in this book are about how you structure your days and work with your own mind, feedback is the lever that multiplies them all. It is a core practice in both your Send It casts and your Tend It & Track rhythms. Time management is more powerful when your team feels safe enough to tell you what's blocking them. Health routines are easier to sustain when colleagues and family respect your boundaries. Meaningful work comes to life faster when you can co-design roles with people you trust. Mental skills are less exhausting when you aren't constantly defending yourself in low-trust relationships.

One helpful companion frame here is The 15 Commitments of Conscious Leadership, which starts with Responsibility and Curiosity—a clean reminder, especially when receiving feedback, to own your part and stay genuinely interested in what you might be missing (Dethmer, Chapman, and Klemp, 2014).

You don't need perfect relationships with everyone, but you do need a critical mass of high-trust connections—people who will tell you the truth and grow with you. Investing in those relationships is not a side project; it is central to a life that is both happy and sustainably effective. Feedback, practiced in small, steady casts, is the most reliable way to build that kind of life.

Chapter 13 – Shaping Your Work

"If you want to fly, you have to give up the things that weigh you down."

—*Toni Morrison*

This chapter is about changing your angle—even when the river (job, company, industry) changes slowly. You may not be able to rewrite your job description tomorrow, but research on "job crafting" suggests we can increase meaning and engagement by shaping work to better fit our strengths and values (Berg, Wrzesniewski, & Dutton, 2010; Wrzesniewski & Dutton, 2001).

Senior leaders often have substantial freedom to craft their roles—but may use that freedom to take on more, rather than to focus. If you're earlier-career or in a more constrained position, you have more agency than you think, especially in the 'cognitive framing' and 'relationships' dimensions.

Job crafting is like adjusting your position on the bank or boat: same water, but different angles, distances, and targets. You'll look at job crafting in three dimensions: 1) Tasks; 2) Relationships; and 3) Cognitive framing. You'll dig into practical tools: role design, values in systems, and calendar design—all ways to align how you spend your time with what you say matters.

This sets you up perfectly for Part IV, where you'll build the Tend It & Track rhythms to keep adjusting your position over time.

C.A.S.T.
Curiosity - Aim - **Send It**- Tend It & Track

Three Dimensions of Job Crafting

Job crafting involves making intentional adjustments across three key dimensions to create a more fulfilling and effective work experience.

Tasks: Delegate or streamline work that's low-value and consistently depleting. Expand or claim tasks that align with your strengths and values. Even a 5–10% shift toward more meaningful work can change your experience. You're not trying to escape every hard or boring task—you're seeking small, deliberate shifts toward the kind of work only you can do and that matters most.

Relationships: Spend more time with people who energize you, minimize unnecessary exposure to toxic dynamics, and clarify expectations and boundaries with key stakeholders. Who you fish with—and how you work together—changes your experience of the same river.

Cognitive Framing: Reframe your work in terms of its impact: whom it serves, what it enables, and why it matters. Connect even routine elements to the larger mission when that connection is honest. This isn't about pretending a bad situation is good; it's about reclaiming agency in how you interpret the work you already have, so your daily casts feel more connected to your Aim.

Four Tools for Shaping Your Work

The three dimensions above give you a lens. Here are four tools I've found especially useful for shifting your work in practice.

They're all examples of **Send It** in action: concrete ways of bringing your values and impact priorities into how you structure your role and your time.

C.A.S.T.
Curiosity - Aim - **Send It** - Tend It & Track

1. Role Design

When considering role design, ask yourself which aspects of your role are most essential to own given your values and priorities for impact, and what you can delegate or let go of. Shift your focus toward more intentional casts that truly require your experience and authority, and work that aligns with your values—such as culture building, developing successors, or sustainability initiatives. Many leaders gradually accumulate responsibilities that no one else wanted. Role design is about pruning and shaping your portfolio so you spend more time on what only you can do in ways that reflect the kind of leader you aspire to be. This is where your earlier work pays off, translating that clarity into action.

2. Values in Systems

You will improve fulfillment for yourself and others by integrating values into your systems, not just your speeches. This means weaving them into hiring and promotion criteria, performance reviews, conflict resolution processes, and recognition systems such as stories and rituals. This is job crafting at the systems level: shaping the environment in which you and others work. It pulls you toward behaviors you say you care about.

Field Story: Values Work at Plow & Hearth

I joined Plow & Hearth as President in 2011. The business was founded on strong values but over the years those values and culture became less clear. When new owners purchased the business in 2010, they were committed to revitalizing the business. Together, we knew we needed a more curious, aggressive, and positive culture. In my first 90 days, I formed a culture committee, fielded surveys, and conducted interviews. We then identified a small set of aspirational values that felt real and worth striving for.

C.A.S.T.
Curiosity - Aim - **Send It**- Tend It & Track

The hard part took years: weaving those values into town halls, training, recognition, and performance reviews. At first, some people saw it as useless soft stuff. Years later, associates would say things like, "I thought the values talk was fluff. Now I see it as the most important part," and "What I valued most was the focus on assuming positive intent."

It reinforced a simple lesson: **values only matter when they show up in practice and decisions.** That embedding takes time, but there is no better time than the present to start.

3. Calendar Design

If your role defines the what, your calendar reveals the when and how much. Together, they tell the truth about your priorities more clearly than any strategy document (Vanderkam, 2010). A useful filter here is the Eisenhower Matrix, which plots tasks across two dimensions: Urgency and Importance. We often let the Urgent (the immediate splashing of the water) crowd out the Important but Not Urgent (the strategic, long-term casts that move the needle). Regularly auditing your calendar is essential—ask yourself what percentage of your week truly reflects your stated values and impact priorities, and where you might be saying yes out of fear, habit, or guilt. Make explicit decisions to protect time for health, family, and deep work, and to remove or redesign meetings and commitments that no longer serve your values or impact goals.

Field Story: Calendar Control as a Proxy for Independence
In my peer forum, a fellow member talked often about "calendar control." At first, I heard it as time management. Over time, I realized he was talking about something deeper: whether his days reflected his values. For me, calendar control became a practical gauge of independence and alignment. When my calendar

matched my values, I felt grounded. When it didn't, it was often a sign I had drifted into other people's priorities.

Leaders who take role and calendar design seriously often find that small structural changes—delegating a major responsibility, blocking focused work time, saying no to one board—have disproportionate effects on both their effectiveness and their sense of freedom.

From a Sight Casting standpoint, job crafting is like adjusting your position on the bank or boat: same water, but different angles, distances, and targets. Calendar design is often where those adjustments become **visible and real**.

4. Values in Daily Framing

The three tools above are largely structural, but there's also a cognitive element: how you talk to yourself about your work. You can support your job crafting efforts by regularly asking where you can act today in a way that's most aligned with your values, by asking, for any given meeting or task, who it serves and why it matters, or if you viewed a particular responsibility through the lens of your Aim, what would shift.

Again, this is not about sugarcoating a bad situation—it's about noticing where your work already connects to what you care about, making that connection more explicit in your own mind, and letting that meaning guide which casts you make and which you let pass. This mental reframing is closely tied to the ACT tools from earlier: noticing your stories about work, holding them lightly, and choosing behavior that serves your values even when the story is "this part of the river is boring" (Hayes et al., 2011).

At this point, you're not just reacting to whatever shows up. You're consciously choosing what you own, how you spend time, and how you interpret the work in front of you. You're moving your feet and giving yourself a better chance to make casts that matter.

Before we shift into the ongoing rhythms of Tend It & Track, there's one more piece to look at: what it actually feels like when all of this comes together at its best. If Curiosity helps you see the water, Aim helps you choose your target, and Send It gets your line on the water—then peak experiences and flow are what it feels like when the cast lands exactly where you meant it to. These moments aren't just rewards; they're compass points that show you what's worth aiming for.

In the next chapter, you'll explore peak experiences and flow—those rare but powerful moments when your skills, your values, your environment, and your attention line up, when work feels deeply absorbing rather than grinding, when time seems to drop away, and when you have the felt sense of "this is exactly where I'm meant to be, doing exactly what I'm meant to be doing."

Chapter 14 – Peak Experiences and Flow

"The best moments in our lives are not the passive, receptive, relaxing times...the best moments usually occur if a person's body or mind is stretched to its limits in a voluntary effort to accomplish something difficult and worthwhile."

—*Mihaly Csikszentmihalyi*

Beyond the daily grind, there are moments on the river and in life when time dissolves, and you become utterly, effortlessly present.

This chapter explores what it feels like when everything comes together at its best—peak experiences and flow states. These moments of deep engagement, intense meaning, and profound connection often define our most cherished memories and contribute significantly to eudaimonic well-being. They are the times when you feel most aware, most effective, and most aligned with your deepest self.

You'll examine what peak experiences and flow are, how they contribute to happiness and fulfillment, and ways to design your life and work to invite more of these moments rather than waiting for chance. While these experiences are not the entirety of a good life, they often serve as bright points that reveal what truly matters and why all the practice is worth it.

C.A.S.T.
Curiosity - Aim - **Send It** - Tend It & Track

Peak Experiences: Moments of Profound Meaning

The concept of peak experiences was introduced by psychologist Abraham Maslow, a pioneer in humanistic psychology. He described them as rare, exciting, oceanic, and exhilarating moments—times when we feel deeply moved and "B-values rich" (Maslow, 1964; see also Chapter 1).

These are not necessarily grand, life-altering events. A peak experience could be a sudden moment of clarity during a complex problem-solving session, a profound connection felt during a conversation with a loved one, or a breathtaking view on a hike. It might be a moment of intense creativity while working on a project, or a feeling of deep peace and belonging in nature.

While brief, they are defined by intense positive emotion—a sense of joy, awe, or profound peace. In a peak experience, you often lose your sense of self-consciousness; you become so fully present that self-awareness fades, replaced by a feeling of unity with the world or the task at hand. Reality seems more vivid, actions feel effortless and spontaneous, and the experience feels intrinsically valuable—an end in itself that needs no external justification.

Ultimately, peak experiences are not about external achievement, but about internal resonance. They are moments when your inner and outer worlds align, and you feel a profound sense of rightness—where your Aim, your actions, and your environment briefly click into place.

Field Story: Wilderness, Risk, and Awe in Alaska

One of my peak experiences came on a trip to Alaska, deep in the wilderness of the Alagnak River area. Friends and I hired outfitters to take us far off the grid. A float plane dropped us at a remote lake with drift boats, and we knew we wouldn't see it again until it picked us up a week later and over 50 miles downstream.

The trip took serious preparation and carried real risk. Once we were in, we were in. What we got in return was a string of peak moments like watching grizzlies and wolves in their home territory, catching huge salmon and rainbow trout in wild water, and coming across a grizzly cache—a half-buried dead caribou carcass—that made the food chain and our place in it feel very immediate.

Those days combined risk, effort, immersion in nature, camaraderie, and a sense of being very small in a very big, very alive world. The experience wasn't just about the number or size of the fish. It was the total experience: preparation, wilderness, wildlife, and the feeling of being exactly where we were meant to be, doing exactly what we were meant to be doing.

That's the texture of a peak experience: not just intensity, but deep resonance with your values—adventure, nature, friendship, mastery, humility in the face of something larger. Looking back, that trip wasn't an escape from the work of leading—it was a reminder of what I was leading *for*. The clarity I brought home shaped decisions for months afterward.

Flow: The State of Optimal Experience

Building on Maslow's work, psychologist Mihaly Csikszentmihalyi (pronounced "Me-high Cheek-sent-me-high") extensively researched the concept of **flow** (Csikszentmihalyi, 1990; see also Chapter 1), which he defined as:"

"A state in which people are so involved in an activity that nothing else seems to matter; the experience itself is so enjoyable that people will do it even at great cost, for the sheer sake of doing it."

Flow is often described as being "in the zone." It's a state of optimal consciousness where you are fully immersed in an

C.A.S.T.
Curiosity - Aim - **Send It** - Tend It & Track

activity, experiencing energized focus, full involvement, and enjoyment in the process of the activity. Flow has a recognizable texture: you know what you're doing and how it's going, the challenge matches your skill, and you're so absorbed that self-awareness drops away. Time bends—hours feel like minutes. The work itself becomes the reward, not what it might earn you later. You're not performing; you're simply present and effective.

Flow is not just about feeling good; it's about **optimal functioning and learning**. When you are in flow, you are often performing at your best and developing your skills.

The Connection Between Peak Experiences and Flow

While distinct, peak experiences and flow are closely related. Sustained periods of flow often culminate in a peak experience—a moment of profound insight or joy that stands out in memory. Both states involve deep engagement; you are fully present and absorbed in what you're doing. **Both are also intrinsically rewarding**: you seek them for their own sake, not for external rewards.

For leaders, understanding these concepts is crucial because they represent the **pinnacle of engagement and fulfillment**. They are the moments when your work feels most meaningful, your contributions most impactful, and your life most vibrant.

Designing for More Peak Experiences and Flow

You don't just wait for these moments to happen. You can actively design your life and work to invite them. Many of the levers you've already seen—structuring your days, shaping your work, using ACT skills to work with your mind—are in service of this.

C.A.S.T.
Curiosity - Aim - **Send It** - Tend It & Track

You can design for more of these moments by working two dimensions:

First, cultivate the conditions for absorption. Flow emerges when you're stretched but not overwhelmed—when challenge matches skill. This is job crafting in service of engagement: adjust what you own, delegate what drains you, and protect blocks for deep work. Peak experiences often happen when you know what you're aiming for and can see progress; this connects directly to your Aim work from Part II. And use the environment design principles from Chapter 13 to minimize distraction. When internal or external noise drops, you create space for full presence.

Second, invite novelty and transcendence. Seek experiences that make you feel small in a good way: time in wild places, new skills, creative risks, moments that connect you to something larger than your current to-do list. These aren't daily occurrences, but they're compass points. When you understand how today's work connects to what matters most, even routine tasks become more absorbing.

Reframe the grind as part of the larger cast you're making (Chapter 7). And use ACT moves (Chapter 9) to return to the moment when your mind drifts to worry or self-criticism. Defusion and contact with the present moment reduce internal noise—the precondition for both flow and peak experiences.

The goal isn't to manufacture peak moments on demand. It's to shape your life so that engagement, meaning, and occasional transcendence become more frequent—and your impact comes from the parts of you that feel most alive.

C.A.S.T.
Curiosity - Aim - **Send It**- Tend It & Track

The Angler's Flow: Beyond the Catch

Think back to the angler. While the catch might be the goal, real "flow" lives in the process: the perfect cast as the line unfurls; the focus of reading water and anticipating where a fish might hold; the absorbed concentration of tying flies; the quiet immersion in a wild place where time disappears.

The Alaska story shows two related kinds of optimal experience. There was flow in the moment-to-moment work of fishing, and a peak experience rooted in wilderness, risk, camaraderie, and awe. Fishing was part of it. The deeper meaning came from immersion in a demanding, beautiful environment with people I cared about.

I could name other peaks, also tied to fishing and adventure, but designed around family. A backcountry trip into the Wind River Range with my oldest son, Drake, when he caught a trophy golden trout in a lake that will stay our secret. A cross-country trip with my youngest son, Cove, when he caught a hog of a rainbow trout on a western creek that will also remain unnamed. In both cases, my boys caught bigger fish than I did. They still don't quite believe I'm glad they did. Their excitement was exactly what I'd hoped those trips would deliver. The fish mattered, but what I remember most is the look on their faces and the quiet knowledge that I'd made a cast that counted.

These moments underline a few points. Peak experiences and flow usually sit on top of long preparation. You can raise the odds, but you will never fully control them. That's part of the magic. Humility and gratitude often accompany peaks.

Peak experiences leave a lasting imprint. They act like a compass, showing you what's possible and what truly resonates. Their memory steadies you in hard seasons. And they nudge you toward growth, reminding you why the daily work matters.

C.A.S.T.
Curiosity - Aim - **Send It** - Tend It & Track

For leaders, the move is simple: design your life and work the way you designed those trips. Commit time and preparation. Accept risk and uncertainty. Immerse yourself in environments that matter. When grand slam moments show up—a transformative project, a breakthrough with a team—you'll recognize them as both earned and gifted. You'll know you made the cast on purpose. You're not chasing fleeting pleasure. You're building a life rich in meaning and engagement where choices crystallize into moments that remind you why you're doing all of this in the first place.

Exercise: Designing for Freshness

You can't manufacture peak moments on demand, but you can design your life to make them more likely. Here's a simple move:

Recall 2–3 deeply rich moments from the last 2–3 years. These might have been trips, creative breakthroughs, deep conversations, or times when you felt fully alive and aligned. For each, ask: Where were you? Who were you with? What were you doing? What values were expressed?

Look for patterns. What ingredients tend to show up during these moments? Risk and preparation? Connection with specific people? Creative challenge? Solitude? Physical effort? Novelty?

Design 2 small experiments for the next 90 days. Think of this as designing "fewer, better casts" of attention to psychological richness. These don't have to be grand—a 24-hour trip with a friend, protected time in a place that matters (Oishi et al., 2020).

The goal isn't to fill your calendar with peak experiences. It's to notice what conditions invite them, and then deliberately create space for those conditions rather than waiting for chance.

(For a more detailed version of this exercise, including reflection prompts and planning templates, see the "Designing Freshness" tool in the Toolkit appendix.)

C.A.S.T.
Curiosity - Aim - **Send It** - Tend It & Track

Key Takeaways from Part III: Send It

Here are the six key takeaways from Part III: Send It:

1. **Make the First Cast Count**: Success hinges on the quality of your start. Focus on preparation and intentionality. Set a high standard that carries through the rest of your work.

2. **Work Skillfully with Your "Inner Weather"**: Use ACT learnings to make room for difficult feelings without letting them drive the boat.

3. **Lead with Recommendations**: Build a culture where everyone feels accountable for providing solutions. Empower every individual to lead.

4. **Build Trust and Normalize Feedback**: High-performing teams rely on psychological safety. Make feedback a routine, non-threatening part of the culture. Create an environment where growth and honesty are the default.

5. **Shape Your Work**: Proactively align responsibilities with strengths and the organization's highest needs to ensure your contribution is both sustainable and high-impact.

6. **Design for Peak Experiences and Flow:** Create conditions where challenge, purpose, and presence converge. Learn from these moments. Use them as compass points for work and leadership that matters most.

Looking Ahead: Tend It & Track

In the final part of the book, you'll look at how to Tend It & Track—the simple check-ins and metrics that ensure your daily actions stay aligned with your long-term aim as the water continues to change.

C.A.S.T.
Curiosity - Aim - **Send It** - Tend It & Track

PART IV: TEND IT & TRACK
Monitoring, Adjusting, and Sustaining

The best cast in the world fails if you don't track the results and adjust. The river changes. The wind shifts. The fish move. You must read the feedback and recalibrate continuously.

Part IV is about building a practice to **Tend It & Track** what matters, recognizing when you're drifting off course, and making the adjustments needed to stay aligned with your values and effective in your leadership.

This is an ongoing practice, a rhythm of observation and adjustment that sustains you through changing circumstances and helps you keep returning to the kind of flow and peak moments you saw in the last chapter.

C.A.S.T.
Curiosity - Aim - Send It - **Tend It & Track**

Chapter 15 – Tracking and Recalibration

"Just as a snake sheds its skin, we must shed our past over and over again."

—*Dalai Lama*

The most effective anglers don't just cast and hope; they watch the water, read the signs, and constantly refine their approach.

You've journeyed through the science of happiness and fulfillment, explored your inner landscape, clarified your values and desired impact, learned practical levers for how you work and relate, and discovered how to invite peak experiences and flow.

Now, the critical question: **How do you sustain this and keep adjusting as the river changes?** This isn't a one-time read or a checklist to complete. It's an ongoing practice, a continuous process of reading the water, adjusting your aim, and making your cast. This chapter is about building a simple, sustainable system for tracking and recalibration—your personal operating rhythm for sustained happiness, fulfillment, and impact.

The Illusion of the Fixed Plan

Life is dynamic. Values, priorities, and circumstances will shift. The idea you can create a perfect, fixed plan and simply execute it indefinitely is an illusion. Instead, think of yourself as a skilled navigator. You have a destination (your values and desired impact), a compass (your core principles), and tools (the levers and ACT skills). But the weather changes, the currents shift, and

C.A.S.T.
Curiosity - Aim - Send It - **Tend It & Track**

new obstacles appear. So, you must keep cycling through the same four moves: observe what's happening, orient yourself relative to where you're trying to go, decide on the best next step, and then act. This cycle—often called the OODA loop (Boyd, 1987)—is a continuous process of observation and adjustment.

Why Track? The Power of Conscious Observation

Tracking isn't about obsessive self-monitoring. It's about conscious observation—bringing awareness to patterns that might otherwise remain unconscious.

Even simple awareness can shift behavior (Clear, 2018; Fogg, 2020). Research on self-monitoring shows tracking behavior increases goal attainment and self-regulation (Harkin et al., 2016; Michie et al., 2009). When you track a few high-leverage indicators, you learn what works for your unique biology, personality, and circumstances. You spot drift early—small deviations from your values or well-being practices can be corrected before they become major problems. And you celebrate progress, which reinforces the behaviors you want to keep.

What to Track: Measurements That Matter

Resist the urge to track everything. Focus on a few high leverage indicators that give a pulse on well-being and alignment. Here is an example of how you could frame five rivers flowing through your life, with a weekly check-in for each:

Energy River (Physical & Mental) - Rate physical energy this week on a scale of 1–10, and do the same for mental clarity and focus. These are foundational markers—when energy is low, it impacts everything else in life and work.

Values River (Alignment)- Reflect on the areas where you felt most aligned with your core values this week and identify where you felt most out of alignment. This serves as your compass check, helping you understand whether you're moving in your chosen direction.

Connection River (Relationships) - Consider whether you felt meaningfully connected to your core relationships this week and whether you made time for the people who matter most. Relationships are a primary driver of well-being, making this reflection essential.

Flow River (Engagement) - Think about when you felt most absorbed, engaged, or "in the zone" this week, and identify which activities brought you a sense of deep satisfaction. These peak and near-peak moments indicate where your skills and challenges align optimally.

Meaning River (Overall Fulfillment) - Taking everything into account, rate your overall sense of fulfillment this week. This holistic check-in captures the bigger picture of how your life feels when all the pieces come together.

A simple journal, a note on your phone, or a recurring calendar reminder can work. The key is consistency and reflection.

Recalibration: Adjusting Your Cast

Tracking without recalibration is just data collection. Recalibration is where you take what you've learned and adjust.

An experienced angler or river guide doesn't just cast or row the same way every time. They are constantly recalibrating based on what the water and conditions are doing.

C.A.S.T.
Curiosity - Aim - Send It - **Tend It & Track**

On moving water in a drift boat, this becomes literal. When you approach a rapid, it's not enough to point the bow downstream and hope. A skilled guide reads the water from a distance, looking for rocks, holes, waves, and subtle changes in current. They position the boat so they can row away from hazards—often with the bow pointing at the danger while the guide rows hard in the opposite direction to softer water, especially around bends. For complex rapids, they'll pull the boat to the bank, walk downstream, and plot a safe line before they commit. Sometimes, they'll let clients walk down the bank while they row an empty boat through the roughest section, reducing risk if something goes wrong.

The point is simple and powerful: you don't wait until you're in the middle of the rapid, with no room to maneuver, to start thinking about what to do. You observe early, position yourself deliberately, and plan your line while you still have options. Your personal tracking and recalibration practice serves the same purpose. Regular reflection is you pulling to the bank to scout—stepping out of the current to see what's coming. Clarifying values and priorities is you choosing your line. Sometimes, "walking the clients around" is the equivalent of taking yourself out of the worst of the chaos—saying no to a misaligned commitment, delaying a nonessential project, or asking for help before you're under water.

How to Recalibrate

Based on your tracking, ask what's working and what's not, then identify one small adjustment for the coming week or month. Also ask whether you're being pulled off course by external events or internal stories. Use your ACT skills: Am I fused with a negative thought? Am I letting regret or worry pull me from the present? Am I acting from fear instead of my values?

C.A.S.T.
Curiosity - Aim - Send It - **Tend It & Track**

Your Personal Operating Rhythm

The frequency of your check-ins and recalibrations is personal. There is no one "right" schedule that works for everyone. What matters is having a rhythm you can sustain—one that keeps you looking up from the river often enough to adjust your line, without becoming another perfectionistic project to fail.

Many organizational systems emphasize this same principle. Gino Wickman's *Traction* (2011) and the Entrepreneurial Operating System (EOS) are built around quarterly priorities ("Rocks"), weekly meetings, and a small set of measurables tracked consistently. The discipline works at the organizational level for the same reason it works personally: regular observation and adjustment beat perfect plans that sit on a shelf.

In the next chapter, I'll introduce the idea of a **personal compass**—a simple personal strategy for the year that pulls this Tend It & Track work into one place. In my own life, that compass has become the backbone of my operating rhythm. Most years, the process begins in December with a **look back**: a brief post-mortem on the year that's ending. I review what happened—where I lived in alignment with my values, where I drifted, what surprised me, and what I learned. Out of that reflection, I start sketching early ideas for the year ahead. In January, I share a draft of my compass with my peer forum and then refine it based on our annual retreat. That personal compass becomes a touchstone for the year: it shapes the questions I ask myself, the way I review my calendar, and the kinds of experiments I run.

Around that yearly reset, I build lighter-weight check-ins. On good weeks, I use a mix of tools—sometimes a simple journal, sometimes prompts from an AI agent, sometimes just a few reflective questions in the notes app on my phone. I don't always hit every day; life happens. But **at least a few times a week**, I'll pause long enough to ask: How's my energy? Where did I feel most aligned with my values? Where am I drifting? Those quick check-ins keep the compass from becoming a document I only revisit once a year.

My **peer forum** adds another facet to this rhythm. We typically meet about eight times a year, and those meetings are natural checkpoints for me to report out: How am I doing relative to what I said mattered? Where am I struggling to live my values? What adjustments am I making based on what the river has thrown at me since we last met? That cadence—daily-ish personal check-ins, periodic forum conversations, and an annual review and reset—has sustained me for years. On top of that, there are always ad hoc moments during the year when a major challenge or opportunity forces a more substantial recalibration. When something big shifts, I'll step back and ask: "Does my compass still fit this season, or do I need to reinterpret or revise it?"

You may find a different rhythm more natural. Some leaders thrive on a structured weekly review, or a short quarterly retreat with themselves, or a standing check-in with a coach or accountability partner. The key isn't to copy my pattern; it's to **design one that fits your life**. Start with something simple you're 80% confident you can keep doing, not an idealized system that collapses by February.

Over time, your personal operating rhythm becomes less about rigid routines and more about a lived habit of looking up, noticing, and adjusting your cast with intention.

C.A.S.T.
Curiosity - Aim - Send It - **Tend It & Track**

Adding Accountability: Don't Row This Stretch Alone

There's one more ingredient that dramatically increases the chances you'll keep tending and tracking over time: **accountability partners**. It is hard to do this kind of inner work and long-term recalibration in isolation. When you are tired, overwhelmed, or discouraged, your own mind will always offer you a story about why today doesn't really matter, why you can skip the review "just this once," or why you should go back to blind casting. Having even one other person who knows what you're working on—and is willing to ask how it's going—changes that conversation.

Over the years, **I've relied on many different forms of accountability**: managers, close friends, partners, executive coaches, therapists, and peers. At different life stages and around different topics, different forms have been most helpful. All of them, in their own way, have helped me notice my drift, reconnect with my values, and keep practicing when it would have been easier to slide back into old patterns. One approach I've found especially powerful—when it's available, and as you saw in my own operating rhythm—is a **peer forum**: a group that meets regularly, often with an annual retreat, where members confidentially share real challenges and support each other.

A well-run peer forum can become a place where you can speak honestly about what's working and what isn't, where you're drifting, and what you're afraid to say out loud. They get to know your values and patterns. They ask hard questions and celebrate small wins. For CEOs and senior leaders, there are formal peer groups (Young Presidents Organization, Vistage, Entrepreneurs Organization, and many regional programs). Some industries have their own vertical-specific forums. Some regions offer leadership

C.A.S.T.
Curiosity - Aim - Send It - **Tend It & Track**

roundtables or cross-company peer groups. The labels and structures differ, but the core function is the same: a confidential circle of peers who help you **keep coming back to who you said you want to be.** That said, it's just one approach—not everyone will have access to, or interest in, a formal forum.

If a peer group isn't practical for you, don't let that stop you. An **accountability partner** can also be a close friend, a trusted colleague, a mentor, an executive coach, or a therapist—ideally someone familiar with values-based work or ACT—who is willing to hold your commitments with you. The key is not their title; it's the **agreement**: "Here's what I'm working on. Here's how I want to tend and track my life. Will you check in with me, ask what I'm noticing, and nudge me when I start to drift?" Even a simple monthly coffee, call, or text exchange—"What did you learn this month? What small adjustment are you making next?"—can keep your practice alive when your own motivation dips.

An **executive coach** can be a particularly smart investment in this space—not necessarily as a forever relationship, but even for a defined season to help you embed these practices. A good coach can help you translate broad ideas into specific experiments, set realistic rhythms, and notice your patterns in real time. Even though I *am* a coach, I still rely on others. At different points in my life, I've leaned on executive coaches, peer forums, friends, mentors, and therapists. Not all at once, but as the river of my own life has changed. Practice is harder than theory. Even coaches benefit from other coaches.

A final, honest acknowledgment: this book—like many coaching and leadership books—offers tools, constructs, and language to support you in ways you can remember. But **remembering to practice these principles in real time is hard.** In the middle of a tense meeting, a family crisis, or a crowded calendar, even the best

C.A.S.T.
Curiosity - Aim - Send It - **Tend It & Track**

frameworks can fly out of your head. This is another place where accountability partners are invaluable. Together, you can simplify and customize the ideas in this book to fit your specific situation and your actual life, trimming them down to a few phrases, cues, or questions that you can realistically carry with you.

The **personal compass** you'll create in the next chapter is one practical, powerful tool to share with an accountability partner. It's designed to be customized—to reflect your values, life stage, and current transitions—and to be memorable enough that you can hold it in your mind and language. You and your accountability partner (or coach, or forum) can refine that compass together, make it simpler, and decide how you'll use it: a check-in question, a word you text each other weekly, a short ritual at the start of each month. The key is to **keep things simple** and use language or cues that you can remember and share easily with your accountability partner(s). When you do that, Tend It & Track stops being just another set of ideas in a book and becomes a shared, lived practice.

Organizational Tend It & Track: Climate Surveys as a Leadership Practice

Just as a skilled angler constantly tends to their line and tracks the subtle movements of the water, effective leaders must tend to the organizational climate and track its health. While personal reflection and individual feedback are crucial, understanding the collective sentiment of your team requires a broader lens. This is where well-designed climate surveys become an invaluable leadership practice, serving as a formal mechanism for Tend It & Track at the organizational level.

Climate surveys, when implemented thoughtfully, offer a structured way to gauge the collective pulse of your organization. They provide a snapshot of employee perceptions, attitudes, and engagement, revealing areas of strength and opportunities for improvement. They become increasingly helpful over time. Establishing a baseline allows you to track trends, which are often more helpful than the absolute scores themselves. Observing shifts in sentiment can provide early warnings or validate the positive impact of new initiatives.

To ensure psychological safety and encourage candid feedback, consider engaging a third party for survey administration. External involvement helps assure anonymity, fostering an environment where employees feel comfortable sharing honest perspectives. Participation rates in these surveys are often a good indicator of trust within the organization; high participation suggests employees believe their voices will be heard and valued.

The power of climate surveys, however, lies not just in collecting data, but in the leadership response. After a survey, it is paramount that leaders communicate overarching themes heard and present a game plan for addressing them. Unaddressed feedback leads to cynicism and lower future participation, undermining the very purpose of the survey. This demonstrates that leadership is listening, values employee input, and is committed to fostering a positive and productive work environment.

When crafting your survey, consider including questions that align with your organizational values and strategic priorities. Beyond standard questions about engagement and satisfaction, a powerful addition is an Employee Net Promoter Score (eNPS) question. A well-phrased eNPS question can provide a clear indicator of overall employee sentiment and loyalty. For example:

How likely are you to recommend [Your Company Name] as a place to work to a friend or colleague? Scale: 0 (Not at all likely) and 10 (Extremely likely).

C.A.S.T.
Curiosity - Aim - Send It - **Tend It & Track**

Other areas you can ask about include communication effectiveness, management support, opportunities for growth, resources, training, work-life balance, and perceptions of fairness and inclusion. Remember, the goal is to gather actionable insights that inform your leadership decisions and help you continually tend to and track the health of your organizational waters.

The Ongoing Journey: A Life of Intentionality

This book is not a destination. It's an invitation to a journey of intentionality, self-awareness, and values-driven action.

You will still face challenges and experience discomfort—days when the river is blown out and the fishing sucks. But now, you have a map—the science of well-being—a compass in your clarified values, a toolkit of practical levers including ACT skills, and a practice of tending and tracking through regular reflection, recalibration, and accountability. You are more equipped to navigate the currents, to find the feeder streams, to appreciate the camaraderie, and to make your cast for a life rich in happiness, fulfillment, and impact—no matter what the water brings.

In the next chapter, you'll bring these pieces together in a concrete way by creating your **personal compass**—a simple, memorable expression of your values and intentions for the year ahead. Think of it as one more way to keep this journey of Tend It & Track alive in real time, so you can keep looking up from the river and making your next cast on purpose.

C.A.S.T.
Curiosity - Aim - Send It - **Tend It & Track**

Chapter 16 – Your Personal Strategy Compass

*"First say to yourself what you would be;
and then do what you have to do."*

—*Epictetus*

As the seasons turn and the river shifts, a true north is invaluable—a single point of reference to guide your next year's cast.

You've gotten curious about your life and leadership as it is—not the airbrushed version (Curiosity). You've clarified what matters most in this season and where you want your casts to land (Aim). You've experimented with making this cast count in real conversations and decisions (Send It), and you've learned at least a little about working with the river inside—your thoughts, emotions, and stories—rather than fighting them (ACT). And in this part of the book, we've been talking about how to Tend It & Track: building rhythms, metrics, and reviews that keep you adjusting instead of drifting. This chapter is about one simple tool for tying all of that together each year: a **personal compass**—your personal strategy statement you can remember and use.

We all start the year with good intentions. New Year's resolutions, long lists of goals, ambitious plans. But for many, these intentions fade by February, lost in the daily grind. The river of email, meetings, and requests speeds up, and whatever clarity we had about our Aim gets buried under the urgent.

C.A.S.T.
Curiosity - Aim - Send It - **Tend It & Track**

Earlier in the book, we talked about **fewer, better casts**—seeing broadly, then choosing where to place this cast of your time, attention, or energy. Annual planning is another version of that same move. You can spray goals in every direction, or you can choose a simple, resonant compass that helps you keep coming back to what matters when things get noisy.

Over the years, I've personally moved from setting detailed, complex monthly targets to focusing on less complex quarterly targets, and eventually to identifying **overarching themes** that deeply resonate with my values. I've found that a blend works best for me: themes that provide direction (Aim), supported by a few key, specific goals and habits (Send It and Tend It & Track).

This chapter explores how to create that kind of overarching theme—which can take the form of a single word, a phrase or even a few phrases and actions to tie it together and act as your **personal compass.**. It's a distilled statement of your deepest intentions, a mental anchor that guides decisions, habits, and reflections all year long. As with everything in this book, I'll share the approach that works for me, but it's just an example. You've seen by now that different people relate differently to tools—depending on personality, stage of life, Enneagram patterns, and the kinds of transitions they're facing. My hope is that this chapter gives you ideas, language, and a framework you can adapt to your own life.

The Power of a Guiding Word or Acronym

A guiding word, phrase, or acronym simplifies complexity, cutting through the noise to your core priorities—re-aiming your casts without a 20-page plan. It **personalizes** your direction, rooting it in your values and life stage rather than someone else's checklist. It **energizes** you as a constant, positive reminder of where you're headed, especially when the river is muddy. And it

C.A.S.T.
Curiosity - Aim - Send It - **Tend It & Track**

integrates the many roles and domains of your life into one portable story about who you're becoming.

Books like *One Word That Will Change Your Life* (Britton, Gordon, & Page, 2013), *The ONE Thing* (Keller & Papasan, 2013), *Aliveness Mindset* (Craven, 2023), *Atomic Habits* (Clear, 2018), *Essentialism* (McKeown, 2014), and *Your Best Year Ever* (Hyatt, 2018) all, in their own way, encourage this kind of intentional narrowing and deepening. Bill George's *True North* (2007) and Stephen Covey's principle-centered leadership (1989) laid groundwork for values-based leadership compasses. Robert Glazer's *The Compass Within* (2025) offers a parable focused on discovering core values for major life decisions—partner, vocation, and community. While core values themselves may remain stable, the Personal Compass here is designed to help leaders identify which values require focus and attention as they navigate different life seasons through the C.A.S.T. framework.

Your guiding word or acronym is one practical way to **Tend It & Track** your **Aim** over a full year. You can design something uniquely yours. Fortitude did that for me in a year that demanded strength and the following section shares that experience.

A Year of Fortitude

For many years, I followed a more traditional approach: I set annual personal goals and tracked progress against my top personal values. Earlier in the book, we walked through a values exercise and looked at how values can guide daily and weekly choices. A couple years ago, a peer group member encouraged us to experiment with the "one word" idea—a way of simplifying all of that into something we could carry around in our heads.

My word for the year was **Fortitude**. I chose Fortitude because I anticipated the year would be challenging. I knew I would be navigating significant caregiving responsibilities, supporting family through hard seasons, and holding a demanding professional life at the same time. I wanted a word that captured strength, endurance, and steadiness under pressure—the same qualities we talked about when we looked at leading through transitions and shocks.

The year was even more challenging than I anticipated. Fortitude proved to be a perfect fit. It became a mantra and North Star—an idea I could return to when I felt exhausted, discouraged, or overwhelmed. In the thickest parts of the year, Fortitude reminded me I could take one more step while staying present and grounded. I could hold the line, even when I couldn't fix everything. In ACT language, it helped me **come back to my values** when my thoughts and feelings were shouting other scripts ("this is too much," "you're failing"). It gave me a way to notice those thoughts, make room for the feelings, and still Send It—still make the next cast that aligned with what I stood for.

As the year wound down and some parts of life began to stabilize, I noticed something shifting in me. Fortitude had been essential, but I didn't want my whole life to be defined by "hanging on" or "enduring." I began to sense that I needed more exploration, moe curiosity, more engagement, the qualities we named earlier in the book as signs of fulfillment, not just survival. I started to ask:

- What does life beyond Fortitude look like?

- If Fortitude helped me survive and stay true through a hard season, what theme might help me thrive in the next one?

- How could I invite more wildness, play, and aspiration into my future without dropping my responsibilities?

C.A.S.T.
Curiosity - Aim - Send It - **Tend It & Track**

Around this time, I also decided to brush off a manuscript I had been working on for a couple of years—focused on living a fulfilling life, especially through transitions. I realized that I was personally in one of those transitional spaces we've talked about: moving from a season of pure endurance to one that could hold both strength and exploration, both responsibility and adventure. As I looked toward the next few years, I knew I wanted a more **aspirational North Star**. Fortitude had been about standing firm in the storm. But, that one word didn't seem like enough. I started to explore more expansive themes that kept the idea of fortitude while adding new mindsets of rising up, exploring, and renewal after the storm. That is the context in which I began to evolve my thinking—drawing on:

- My personal values (from the earlier values work you've done in this book),
- My Enneagram profile and personality tendencies (the temperamental patterns we explored earlier),
- The work of authors like Britton, Gordon, Page, Keller, Papasan, Craven, Clear, McKeown, and Hyatt, and
- The metaphors that were quietly shaping my inner life, especially for exploration and release.

Eventually, through a lot of reflection and refinement, I arrived at a new word and acronym—**S.O.A.R.**—to guide the next season of my life. In terms of defining S.O.A.R., each letter represents a mindset where I want to focus moving forward:

S = Steady Fortitude – I remain grounded and steady even as I release control.

O = Outward Exploration – I will actively seek to engage with the unknown, new experiences, and new depth to relationships.

A = Allow – I guide without gripping, influence without over-controlling, and trust the process.

R = Resolute Impact – I will translate values into action: clear priorities, clear choices, clean follow-through.

S.O.A.R. didn't emerge from thin air. It came from working through the same process I'm about to share with you—a structured reflection on my values, my relationships, my life context, my growth edges, and where I wanted my presence to land in this season. You can see my complete Personal Compass—the raw material, values work, and commitments that led to S.O.A.R.—in the appendix. For now, know that the framework you're about to learn is the same one I used to move from Fortitude (surviving a hard season) to S.O.A.R. (releasing control while inviting more aliveness into the next season of my life). In the pages that follow, I will offer you the process I used to arrive at S.O.A.R. so you can craft your own **personal compass**.

Building Your Personal Compass: A 5-Step Process

This isn't about finding the perfect word, phrase or acronym. It's about landing on something honest and workable for you. Once a year, this is your way of returning to the same core questions we've been asking: Who am I at my best? What matters most right now? How do I want to show up in my Send It moments? How will I remember and course-correct when I drift?

The steps that follow walk you, step by step, through creating your own version.

C.A.S.T.
Curiosity - Aim - Send It - **Tend It & Track**

Step 1: Gather Raw Material – Who Are You, What's Emerging?
Before you can distill, you need to collect. This step is about honest self-assessment about what is already true about you, and what is pressing on you right now. You can draw from:

*Your Core Values***:** Earlier, you identified the 4–5 non-negotiable principles that matter most. Revisit them. What matters to you *now*? Which values feel most threatened?

*Your Personality / Tendencies / Strengths***:** Recall patterns we explored in the Curiosity section—your typical ways of striving, defending, connecting. What are your default patterns, gifts, and challenges? Where do you tend to over-function, over-accommodate, over-achieve, or overanalyze?

Your Life Context & Roles: What realities shape this coming year (work, family, health, community, financial pressures, transitions)? Think in "domains" the way we did when we mapped roles earlier in the book.

Your Growth Edges & Desires: Where are you stretched or called to grow next? What kind of leader, partner, parent, friend, or citizen, do you want to become on the other side of this year?

This is in the spirit of mindsets we discussed when we talked about identity and transitions: starting with how you want to show up, especially under pressure, not just what you want to accomplish.

Step 2: Identify 3–4 Core Focus Areas for the Coming Year
Based on your raw material, name **3–4 values-based domains or mindsets** that matter most for the next chapter. These are not just goals; they're ways of being that will shape your goals and habits.

For each area, write 1–2 sentences: 1) "When I'm at my best in this area, I..." and 2) "In the coming year, I want to grow by..."

C.A.S.T.
Curiosity - Aim - Send It - **Tend It & Track**

Possible areas might include:

- Physical health / endurance
- Emotional steadiness / resilience
- Relationships / caregiving / parenting
- Work / leadership / contribution
- Adventure / fun / renewal
- Inner work / spirituality / reflection
- Transition / reinvention / legacy

In one planning cycle, this step led me to themes like:

- Carrying forward the best of **Fortitude**,
- More immersive, **Outward Exploration**,
- **Allowing** more and gripping less, and
- **Resolute Impact** in how I show up for family, friends, clients, and rivers.

If you've been tracking metrics (energy, alignment, connection, flow) as suggested in Tend It & Track, those can also inform focus areas. Where did you feel most alive? Most drained? That's data.

Step 3: Explore Guiding Words or an Acronym

Now you are ready to name the pattern. You have several options: choosing a single guiding word, selecting themes, or creating a short acronym where each letter represents one of your casting mindsets. These could be values-based or other guiding principles that help focus. For example, my emerging framework became S.O.A.R., with each letter later defined as a particular area of focus.

To explore this, **start by brainstorming words and phrases that resonate with your focus areas**. Revisit metaphors and images that have been meaningful. Throughout this book, we've used sight-casting as a central metaphor, but you may have your own—mountains, music, parenting, building, gardening, and so on.

In my case, falconry unexpectedly became central. My son is a falconer, and over the past few years, I learned a tremendous amount from him. Hawks and accipiters don't respond to force or negative reinforcement; they respond to trust, consistency, and food-based positive reinforcement. You don't control a hawk; you invite its cooperation. That requires preparation, patience, and letting go of control—exactly what I was working on in my life.

Those experiences pulled me toward images of flight, release, and return—not just holding on (Fortitude) but lifting off. It was another version of the same Send It decision: do I grip harder, or do I make a cleaner, more trusting cast? As you brainstorm, notice which words keep showing up in your journal, your conversations, and your imagination. Pay attention to which word feels like both a home and a horizon. For me, S.O.A.R. emerged as the word that could hold all of this: the Fortitude I still needed, the Exploration I craved, the Allowing I needed to practice, and the Impact I wanted to have.

Step 4: Iterate and Listen for Resonance

Arriving at your word or theme is often a gradual process. It may take days or weeks of circling around a few candidates. You might journal about each contender, asking, "If this were my theme for the year, what would change? What would stay the same?"

Pay attention to your body and your gut. Does this theme feel like a burden, a performance, a mask? Or does it feel like an honest, challenging, hopeful description of who you're becoming?

With Fortitude, I felt a deep sense of truth and necessity. With S.O.A.R., I felt a sense of invitation and possibility. The shift from one to the other matched the shift I felt internally—from surviving

C.A.S.T.
Curiosity - Aim - Send It - **Tend It & Track**

a hard season to asking, "What kind of life do I want to build on the other side of this?"

If you've practiced ACT concepts from earlier, you can use those here too. Notice stories and emotions each candidate word brings up. Your word, theme, or acronym doesn't have to feel comfortable; it must feel true and helpful.

Step 5: Tighten the Framework

Once you've chosen your guiding idea, bring it down from concept into daily life—into actual casts. For each theme, word or phrase, you can write a description about what it means to you. You could also expand this concept by writing 2–4 concrete behaviors or commitments for each mindset or priority to help guide how you will show up in your calendar and choices.

By doing this work, you're not just naming a theme; you're writing your personal compass or any other way you want to label this work in plain language. It becomes one more way of making your identity about **values and ways of being** than about any single role or achievement, as we discussed in the identity chapter. If you want to see this entire process in action—from Curiosity questions through values clarification to specific commitments and a guiding framework—turn to the appendix. I've included my complete 2026 Personal Compass as a worked example. It shows how I moved from reflecting on the past year (what worked, what didn't, where I felt most alive and engaged) to identifying my core values (health, empathy, independence, sustainability, responsibility) to landing on S.O.A.R. as my guiding framework. Your compass will look different—different values, different seasons, different commitments—but the process is the same. The appendix tool includes both a blank template and my completed example so you can see exactly how the pieces fit together.

C.A.S.T.
Curiosity - Aim - Send It - **Tend It & Track**

Your Personal Compass in Action

At this point, you have what you need: a simple, memorable construct that holds your values, context, and intentions in one place. It connects to everything you've done in this book. It grows out of **Curiosity** about who you are and where you are in life. It clarifies your **Aim** for this season. It guides how you **Send It** in specific conversations, projects, and decisions. It gives you discipline to **Tend It & Track** progress.

Fortitude carried me through a year that demanded strength. S.O.A.R. is inviting me into a season that demands strength plus openness, courage plus curiosity, release instead of control, responsibility plus exploration.

Your life will still be complex. But your orientation can be simple. Print your framework and keep it visible—on your desk, in your journal, as a starting point for quarterly reviews. Return to the Personal Compass tool in the appendix to help you reset once a year, then return to it quarterly to ask:

- Where am I in the C.A.S.T. framework right now?

- What does my compass say?

- And what would it look like to **make this next cast count**?

C.A.S.T.
Curiosity - Aim - Send It - **Tend It & Track**

Key Takeaways from Part IV: Tend & Track

Part IV is where you built a **Personal Compass** and an operating rhythm to ensure your values don't get buried by the urgent and drift off course. Here are the four core takeaways:

1. **Recalibrate and Design a Sustainable Rhythm**: Build a personal operating rhythm—perhaps an annual reset, weekly reflections, and periodic deep dives—that keeps you looking up from the work often enough to adjust your line without becoming a perfectionistic burden.

2. **Don't Row Alone**: Accountability is the engine of change. Whether through a peer forum, a coach, or a trusted friend, having someone who knows your Aim and is willing to nudge you when you drift is essential. Practice is harder than theory; even the best guides need a second set of eyes on the water.

3. **Anchor in Your Personal Compass**: Distill your values and current life stage into a simple, memorable personal compass—a single word, phrase, or acronym (like *Fortitude* or *S.O.A.R.*). This acts as a mental anchor for your decisions, helping you stay aligned with who you want to be even when the water gets muddy.

Looking Ahead: The Final Cast

With Part IV, you now have a way to keep this work alive in real time. Next, you'll zoom out to the book's conclusion, integrating Curiosity, Aim, Send It, and Tend & Track into one cohesive way of leading and living.

C.A.S.T.
Curiosity - Aim - Send It - **Tend It & Track**

CONCLUSION: FORWARD C.A.S.T.

The river you stand in today won't be the same six months from now, and neither will the leader you are. This isn't a problem to solve—it's the condition of a well-lived life. If you've read this far, you're not after quick fixes or easy answers. You're seeking a rhythm you can hold in the current, grounded in evidence, honest about tradeoffs, and worthy of the responsibilities you carry.

You've learned to see the water more clearly (Curiosity), aim with precision (Aim), step with better technique (Send It), and adjust as conditions change (Tend It & Track). You've built a Personal Compass—a personal strategy that helps you re-aim each year, carrying values, context, and intentions into the next season. This is the C.A.S.T. framework. It's a practice you'll return to again, evolving with the river and yourself. The work is never "done." That's not a flaw—it's a feature. **It's what leads to a life of intentionality, impact, and fulfillment** instead of over-casting for achievement, under-aiming your life, carrying a culture that brings you problems, or drifting without a compass.

CORE INSIGHTS

Here are the key lessons to carry with you.

Happiness isn't the absence of difficulty; it's the presence of meaning. Leaders don't seek constant pleasure; they build lives where effort matters, and discomfort is the price of admission.

Your baseline isn't your destiny. Genetics and temperament matter, but so do circumstances and intentional action. Wisdom lies in knowing what you can change—and what you must accept.

C.A.S.T.
Curiosity - Aim – Send It - Tend It & Track

Peak experiences and flow are leadership fuel. These moments of deep engagement sustain you. They aren't distractions; they're often what "the work" looks like when it's done well.

Self-awareness is foundational. You can't change what you don't see. Personality tools, reflection, and honest feedback become essential infrastructure for effective leadership.

Values-driven action beats willpower. You don't need to feel ready to act on your values—clarity and commitment make hard choices easier.

The shift from achievement to impact changes everything. Impact is ongoing and relational, pushing you to ask "What difference have I made?" instead of "What have I accomplished?"

This work requires infrastructure, not just motivation. Peer groups, mentors, partners, friends, coaches, rituals, and your Personal Compass are vital support options for sustainable leadership.

THE C.A.S.T. JOURNEY

You've walked through the four parts of this book as distinct sections, but C.A.S.T. is not a linear checklist. It's a loop. You keep circling through Curiosity, Aim, Send It, and Tend & Track—seeing more clearly, choosing more wisely, acting more skillfully, and adjusting more intentionally as the river changes.

C.A.S.T.
Curiosity - Aim - Send It - Tend It & Track

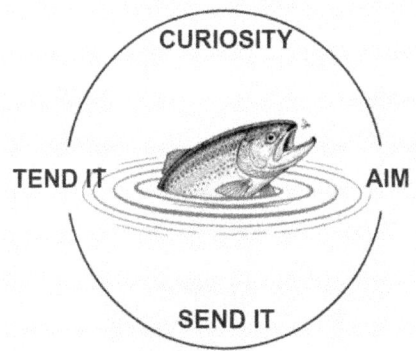

The C.A.S.T. Framework

Curiosity: See What's True

In Part I, you learned to see the water you're in. You focused on pillars of well-being like relationships, meaningful work, community, novelty, and health. You named personality patterns: where you over-function, over-achieve, or overanalyze.

Curiosity means you keep looking honestly at your life and patterns. Revisit your personality profile or feedback periodically. Notice life-stage transitions. Ask a few trusted people, "What do you see me overusing? Where do I get in my own way?" Curiosity is how you stop blind casting and **rebalance where you are over-functioning in some areas while under-aiming in others.**

Aim: Choose What Matters Now

In Part II, you turned seeing into direction. You clarified values as a lived compass, not a branding exercise. You looked at your wake—how your presence lands on people and systems. You loosened your grip on identity as a set of titles and roles and anchored it more in values that travel with you.

To keep your Aim true, return to your values regularly. Ask, "Given this season, what's a good use of me, here, now?" Notice

C.A.S.T.
Curiosity - Aim - Send It - Tend It & Track

where achievement-for-its-own-sake starts to creep back in and gently redirect toward meaningful impact. As your life changes, let your Aim evolve with it, **so you're no longer aiming the business with precision while aiming your own life by default.**

Send It: Act and Lead with Intention

If you remember only one thing from Send It, let it be this: **Build a culture of trust, normalized feedback, and accountability to lead with recommendations.** Everything else in Send It is in service of that. When trust is high and feedback is routine and safe, people at every level feel responsible for offering a clear point of view—not just asking, "What should I do?" but saying, "Here's what I recommend and why." That is the leadership shift **from carrying a culture that brings you problems to leading a culture that owns solutions.**

Acceptance and Commitment Therapy (ACT) and structure are scaffolding that make this possible. Working with your "inner weather" (ACT) helps you stay grounded to receive hard feedback, give it cleanly, and invite recommendations instead of controlling every answer. Structuring your day and shaping work creates space and energy to invest in relationships, prepare for key conversations, and be present to build psychological safety.

Tend It & Track: Your Personal Compass Anchors the Rest

In Part IV, you learned to keep looking up from the river. You defined a small set of things to notice—energy, values alignment, connection, engagement, fulfillment—and you built a rhythm of reflection and adjustment. At the center of that work is your Personal Compass. If you do only one thing from Tend It & Track, make it this: Create and use a simple compass.

C.A.S.T.
Curiosity - Aim - Send It - Tend It & Track

That compass is the anchor. Once it's clear, the rest of your tracking becomes easier and lighter: weekly or bi-weekly check-ins asking, "How am I doing relative to this compass?" A brief annual reset. Periodic conversations with a coach, forum, or trusted friend who knows your compass and can ask how you're living it.

The point isn't to monitor everything; it's to notice drift early and realign—**so you don't look up in five years and realize you've been drifting on a life you didn't mean to build.**

Why This Work Matters

This isn't self-indulgent work. It's stewardship—the inner work that lets you stay effective, ethical, and human in roles that demand a lot and forgive little. The frameworks and tools matter, but the heart of it is simpler: showing up, telling yourself the truth, and choosing values over comfort in mostly unseen moments.

If you remember only a handful of moves, let them be these:

- See your life and patterns honestly (Curiosity).

- Aim your energy at what truly matters now (Aim).

- Build a culture based on leading with recommendations, trust, and feedback. Use ACT and structure to keep showing up that way (Send It).

- Let a Personal Compass anchor a rhythm of tending, so you recalibrate instead of drifting (Tend It & Track).

That's the practice. That's the river. You don't control the current. You do control the cast. Choose well.

C.A.S.T.
Curiosity - Aim - Send It - Tend It & Track

TOOLKIT

Walk into a fly shop and you don't buy everything on the wall—you pick a few pieces of gear that match a river and season. That's how to use this Toolkit. Choose what fits where you are right now, try it, keep what works, and leave the rest. This isn't about turning yourself into a project of self-improvement. It's about getting a few tools from the C.A.S.T. framework that are helpful for you. Some tools help you see more clearly (Curiosity). Some help you decide what matters most now (Aim). Some help you act on purpose under pressure (Send It). And some help you stay aligned over time, so you don't drift (Tend It & Track). Try a couple of tools. Run them for two weeks. Then, recalibrate.

You can find a printable version of these tools online at SightCastingConsulting.com or SightCastBook.com.

The Five Core Tools

1. **Values, Impact, and This Season of Life**
   Clarify core values, how they express in this season of life, and what kind of impact you want to have over the next 3–10 years. This is your **internal compass** for Aim.

2. **Calendar & Commitments Audit**
   Compare your values and desired impact to how you spend your time. Identify what needs to be **removed, reduced, or redesigned**—and what needs **protecting**.

3. **Saying No as Stewardship**
   Use three simple filters (values, impact, season) and a few ready-made scripts to decline or reshape requests in a way that protects your health, your family, and your existing commitments—without unnecessary guilt.

C.A.S.T.
Curiosity - Aim - Send It - Tend It & Track

4. **Designing "Freshness": Peak Moments & Psychological Richness**
   Reflect on your own peak or deeply rich experiences, then design small, values-aligned **new experiences** that bring energy, learning, and perspective into this season.

5. **ACT Mini-Check: Thoughts, Feelings, Values, Action**
   A simple 10-minute reflection you can use when you feel stuck or overwhelmed. Helps you **notice what's going on inside you**, reconnect with your **values**, and choose one **small, committed action**.

In-the-Moment Field Checklist

While the tools above are for reflection and planning, this checklist is for the heat of the moment. It is a one-page guide to help you steady yourself and choose your next cast intentionally during difficult conversations, high-stakes decisions, or emotionally charged situations.

Personal Compass Template

At the end of this Toolkit, you'll also find a **1-page Personal Compass template**—a one-page annual "strategy statement" that pulls your values, impact, and this season of life into a single, portable guide for the year.

C.A.S.T.
Curiosity - Aim - Send It - Tend It & Track

Values and Impact Exercise

Purpose - To clarify what matters most **now**, in this season of your life—so you have a clear internal compass for your choices.

5 Core Values

Core Value # 1 - _____

- For me this value means:
  _____

- I can live this by:
  _____

Core Value # 2 - _____

- For me this value means:
  _____

- I can live this by:
  _____

Core Value # 3 - _____

- For me this value means:
  _____

- I can live this by:
  _____

Core Value # 4 - _____

- For me this value means:
  _____

C.A.S.T.
Curiosity - Aim – Send It - Tend It & Track

- I can live this by:

  _____

Core Value # 5 - _____

- For me this value means:

  _____

- I can live this by:

  _____

* Examples of Values Authenticity, Achievement, Adventure, Autonomy, Balance, Boldness, Compassion, Challenge, Citizenship, Community, Competency, Contribution, Creativity, Curiosity, Determination, Fairness, Faith, Friendships, Fun, Growth, Happiness, Honesty, Humor, Independence, Influence, Justice, Kindness, Knowledge, Leadership, Learning, Loyalty, Meaningful Work, Openness, Optimism, Peace, Play, Pleasure, Poise, Popularity, Recognition, Religion, Reputation, Respect, Responsibility, Security, Self-Respect, Service, Spirituality, Stability, Success, Status, Trustworthiness, Wealth, Wisdom.

Calendar & Commitments Audit

Purpose - To see where your **time and energy** are actually going—and to bring them closer to what you say matters.

Instructions (30–45 minutes)

1. Print or view your last 2–4 weeks of calendar and major commitments.
2. Using three colors or symbols, mark each block or major activity on your calendar as:
    - A – **Aligned** with your values and desired impact
    - N – **Neutral / maintenance** (necessary but not inspiring)
    - D – **Draining / misaligned**
3. Estimate rough percentages of your time:
    - Aligned: ____ %
    - Neutral/maintenance: ____ %
    - Draining/misaligned: ____ %
4. For the **D** category, ask:
    - "Which of these can be **removed, reduced, or redesigned** in the next 90 days?"
    - Circle 1–3 changes that are realistic this quarter.
5. For the **A** category, ask:
    - "Where do I want **more time**?"
    - Identify 1–2 blocks of time you can **protect** more fiercely.
6. Commit to **one calendar change** you will make in the next 30 days:
    - "I will stop/reduce/redesign: ____"
    - "I will protect: ____"

This is where Aim starts to show up on your calendar.

C.A.S.T.
Curiosity - Aim - Send It - Tend It & Track

SAYING "NO" as Stewardship Filters

Purpose - To treat "no" (or "not now/not me") as your responsibility to yourself and to people depending on you.

Three Filters for Vetting Requests

Before you say yes to a new request, quickly run it through filters, if it fails any, then consider a no, reshape, or delay.

1. **Values** - "Is this aligned with my top values for this season?"

2. **Impact** - "Does this meaningfully advance the impact I said I care about in Tool 1?"

3. **Season** - "Given my current life stage and load, does this fit now, or would it crowd out something more important?"

Sample Scripts (adapt as needed)

1. **Clean No – Values / Impact** - "Thank you for thinking of me. Given what I'm focusing on this year, I'm going to say no so I can stay committed to [X]."

2. **No for This Season** - "This is the kind of thing I'd normally say yes to, but this season I've committed to protecting time for [family/health/board work/elder care]. I need to decline so I can keep that promise."

3. **Reshape the Ask** - "I can't own this in the way you're describing. What I *could* do...if that would still be useful."

4. **Delay with Intent** - "Right now my plate is full. Could we revisit this in a month?"

Use or rewrite 1–2 of these so they sound like you. Keep them handy so you can **Send It** cleanly in the moment.

C.A.S.T.
Curiosity - Aim - Send It - Tend It & Track

"Designing Freshness" Exercise

Purpose - To deliberately invite more moments of engagement, learning, connection, or awe, without blowing up your life.

> **Recall 2-3 peak or deeply rich moments from the last 2-3 years. For each:**

Experience #1

- Where were you: _____
- Who were you with (if anyone): _____
- What were you doing: _____
- What values were expressed: _____

Experience #2

- Where were you: _____
- Who were you with (if anyone): _____
- What were you doing: _____
- What values were expressed: _____

C.A.S.T.
Curiosity - Aim - Send It - Tend It & Track

Experience #3

- Where were you:
  _____

- Who were you with (if anyone):
  _____

- What were you doing:
  _____

- What values were expressed:
  _____

Look for patterns. "What *ingredients* tend to be present during these moments?"

What ingredients tend to be present during these moments:

- _____

- _____

- _____

Freshness Activities - Design 2 small experiments for the next 90 days.

Design a couple small activities that will add some novelty or depth or awe to your days.

Experiment #1

- Where will you go/be:
  _____

- Who will you be with (if anyone):
  _____

- What will you do:
  _____

- What values will be expressed:
  _____

Experiment #2

- Where will you go/be:
  _____

- Who will you be with (if anyone):
  _____

- What will you do:
  _____

- What values will be expressed:
  _____

Examples: A 24-hour overnight trip with a close friend or partner to a {xx place} to connect and express friendship and empathy.

Check In – Acceptance and Commitment Therapy (ACT)

Purpose: To give you a quick, repeatable check—thoughts, feelings, values, action—so you can regain clarity when you're stuck and act in line with what matters, now and over time.

Instructions: Use the "ACT Check" for immediate clarity when feeling stuck or overwhelmed. Integrate it into the "Periodic Alignment Check-In" for broader reflection and course correction.

ACT Check (In-the-Moment)

(Use when feeling stuck, flooded, or off-center. ~5 minutes.)

1. **Situation:** Briefly describe a challenge (1-2 sentences).

2. **Thoughts (Noticing):** What thoughts is your mind giving you? (e.g., "I'm having the thought that I'm failing.")

3. **Feelings (Allowing):** What sensations are you noticing in your body? Can you make room for them for 60 seconds?

4. **Values (Remembering):** Which 1-2 values do you most want to embody in this situation? (e.g., "In this moment, I care about courage and connection.")

5. **Action (Choosing):** What is one small action you can take in the next 24 hours that moves you 1% more in the direction of those values? (Make it tiny and observable.)

Periodic Alignment Check-In - *(Reflect and plan. Aim for 15-20 minutes.)*

Month / Year: _____

- **Values Focus:**

    o Top 2–3 values I want to lean into this month:
    _____

    o One small way I will live each value:

        ▪ Value 1 → Action:
        _____
        _____

        ▪ Value 2 → Action:
        _____
        _____

- **Time & Commitments:**

    o This past month, my time felt: Aligned ____% | Neutral ____% | Draining ____%

    o One thing I will stop, reduce, or redesign next month:
    _____

C.A.S.T.
Curiosity - Aim - Send It - Tend It & Track

- **Freshness & Relationships:**
    - One new or meaningful experience I will create next month (What/With Whom/Why):
        - _____
        _____
        _____
    - One relationship I will invest in more intentionally next month (Who/How):
        _____

- **ACT Reflection:**
    - A situation where I felt stuck or challenged:
        _____
        _____
    - Key thoughts/feelings noticed:
        _____
        _____
    - Values I chose to lean on:
        _____
        _____
    - One committed action taken (or to take):
        _____
        _____

C.A.S.T.
Curiosity - Aim - Send It - Tend It & Track

In The Moment: Field Checklist

4 Steps for Leading with Recommendations
- Situation Assessment
- Alternatives
- Recommendation & Why
- Next Steps and Implications

2 Steps When Emotions Arise (ACT)
- Name the Thought
- Recognize emotional impact but act based on values

Framework and Common Language for Role Clarity (RACI)
- Who is the 1 person <u>responsible</u> (only 1)
- Who is/are the <u>approver/decision maker</u>(s)
- Who needs to be <u>consulted</u>
- Who needs to be <u>informed</u>

Trust Equation:
Trust = Credibility + Reliability + Vulnerability / Self-Orientation

How to Give Feedback
- Name the behavior observed (do not question intent)
- Name the impact on you or others
- Name what you need or want

How to Invite / Receive Feedback
- Ask – What can I start/stop/continue to be more effective
- Mirror back what you heard and ask for examples if not provided
- Align on what matters most
- Thank them, commit, and follow up

C.A.S.T.
Curiosity - Aim - Send It - Tend It & Track

Personal Compass – Curiosity, Aim, Send It, and Tend It & Track

NAME: _____ YEAR: _____

1. Curiosity – What did I learn about myself over the past 6-12 months.

- When was I most happy and why:

  _____

  _____

- What disappointed me this past year in terms of my behavior/actions:

  _____

  _____

- When was I at my best and why:

  _____

  _____

- What did I learn about fulfillment that I could do a better job acting upon:

  _____

  _____

2. Aim - Core Values for This Year

Value 1: _____

- In action, this means:
  _____

Value 2: _____

- In action, this means:
  _____

Value 3: _____

- In action, this means:
  _____

Value 4: _____

- In action, this means:
  _____

Value 5: _____

- In action, this means:
  _____

3. Aim - Where I Want My Casts to Land

Here are a few areas where I want my presence to have an impact:

- For **people** (family, team, clients, community):

  _____

  _____

- For **systems / organizations** (companies, boards, teams):

  _____

  _____

- For **places** (communities, rivers, schools, ecosystems):

  _____

  _____

Short impact statement: "In this season, I want my presence to..."

_____

_____

4. Send - Commitments for the Year

Concrete commitments to keep you oriented to your compass.

#1: _____

- Frequency / Timing: _____

#2: _____

- Frequency / Timing: _____

#3: _____

- Frequency / Timing: _____

C.A.S.T.
Curiosity - Aim - Send It - Tend It & Track

5. Send - This Year's "No List"

To protect my compass, I am **intentionally saying no** to:

- _____
- _____
- _____

(Examples: "New for-profit board seats," "Non-mission-aligned speaking invitations,")

6. Guiding Word, Theme, or Acronym for This Year

- My guiding word, theme or acronym:
  _____

In 1–3 sentences, describe what this means for you in this season: "For me, this means…"

- _____
- _____
- _____

7. Track - Simple Review Plan

When and how I will revisit this Personal Compass (weekly, monthly, quarterly):

_____
_____

One question I'll use each time I review it: "In the last month/quarter, where did I live this Compass, where did I drift?"

C.A.S.T.
Curiosity - Aim - Send It - Tend It & Track

Example: John's Personal Compass

Curiosity – What did I learn last year

I was happiest in wild places—fly fishing out west, hiking in the Tetons, and working alongside my son to train hawks.

I over-controlled family situations. I tried to manage outcomes I couldn't control, which drained me and didn't help anyone. I let professional networking slide when I was exhausted.

I was at my best when I showed up for family, holding difficult client conversations with honesty and empathy, and maintaining my fitness routine even when everything else felt chaotic. Fortitude worked.

I could do a better job realizing fulfillment comes from presence, not performance. I need more exploration, more wildness, and more trust in others' paths. I can't just endure—I need to invite more engagement and excitement into my life.

Aim – Core Values for This Year

Health: Sustainable strength—training consistently, honoring recovery, building renewable energy, not burning out.

Empathy: Listening deeply, assuming positive intent, creating space for others' agency and dignity, in caregiving and coaching.

Independence: Protecting time for exploration, solitude, and family; being selective with client engagements.

Sustainability: Connecting with natural places; supporting conservation work; living in ways that honor ecosystems I love.

C.A.S.T.
Curiosity - Aim - Send It - Tend It & Track

Responsibility: Showing up consistently for family, clients, and community; telling the truth clearly.

Aim – This Season I Want Impact…

For people: My family (support while allowing agency), my clients (honest feedback, deeper capability-building).

For systems/organizations: My coaching practice (expand impact with C.A.S.T. framework), peer forums (contribute meaningfully), and organizations I advise (ask hard questions, facilitate growth).

For places: Rivers I care about (conservation work), wild places in the West (spend meaningful time there annually), and my community (civic engagement, environmental stewardship).

Short impact statement: I want my presence to provide stability (not control) and joy for family, strengthen my clients' capability, and protect wild places—with empathy and backbone.

Send It – Commitments for the Year

Train for and complete a spring triathlon: Swim, row, bike, run, 5x/week; Pilates or weights 2x/week; race in spring/summer

Spend time in wild places: Spend at least 3 weeks out west; hike to Teton saddle; practice falconry with son through spring.

Support Parents: Monthly visits and daily calls to check in.

Professional outreach: Networking at least once a week.

Send It – This Year's "No List"

To protect my compass, I am intentionally saying no to new non-profit board seats, speaking invitations that don't align with my coaching work, and over-managing family situations. I will model behavior and influence, not control; I will trust others' paths.

Guiding Theme for This Year

S.O.A.R. links to my values and works on two levels. The word itself serves as mantra and captures imagery of lifting, releasing, and thriving. At the same time, each letter names an intentional mindset:

- **Steady Fortitude** (grounded strength while releasing control)
- **Outward Exploration** (engage in the unknown—wild places, new experiences, deeper relationships)
- **Allow** (guide without gripping; influence without over-controlling, trust the process)
- **Resolute Impact** (translate values into action: clear priorities, clear choices, clean follow-through)

Tend It & Track Plan

I will revisit this Personal Compass monthly as I plan for and participate in my monthly peer group meetings.

Your Personal Compass will reflect your values, your season of life, and your growth edges. Use this example as a guide, not a template. The goal is to create something honest, workable, and memorable—a compass you'll use, not a document that sits in a drawer.

C.A.S.T.
Curiosity - Aim - Send It - Tend It & Track

ADDITIONAL EXPLORATORY

This book draws on rigorous research, but the science of well-being and leadership is vast. The resources below offer accessible, practice-oriented entry points for leaders who want to go deeper. This is not an exhaustive list—it's a curated starting point.

Science and Perspectives on Happiness and Well-Being
- Ed Diener – Happiness: Unlocking the Mysteries of Psychological Wealth
- Sonja Lyubomirsky – The How of Happiness
  Martin Seligman – Flourish
- Mihaly Csikszentmihalyi – Flow
- His Holiness the Dalai Lama & Howard Cutler – The Art of Happiness
- Susan David – Emotional Agility
- Russ Harris – The Happiness Trap

Work, Leadership, and Performance
- Patrick Lencioni – The Five Dysfunctions of a Team
- Shawn Achor – The Happiness Advantage
- Adam Grant – Give and Take; Think Again
- Carol Dweck – Mindset: The New Psychology of Success
- Daniel Goleman – Emotional Intelligence
- Daniel Pink – Drive: The Surprising Truth About What Motivates Us
- Amy Edmondson – The Fearless Organization
- Kerry Patterson et al. – Crucial Conversations

Meaning, Impact, and Later-Career Transitions
- Arthur Brooks – From Strength to Strength; Build the Life You Want
- David Brooks – The Second Mountain
- William Bridges – Transitions: Making Sense of Life's Changes

C.A.S.T.
Curiosity - Aim - Send It - Tend It & Track

- Viktor Frankl – Man's Search for Meaning
- Bill George – True North
- Marshall Goldsmith – What Got You Here Won't Get You There
- Dacher Keltner – Awe

Habits, Behavior Change, and Practical Tools
- James Clear – Atomic Habits
- BJ Fogg – Tiny Habits
- Angela Duckworth – Grit: The Power of Passion and Perseverance
- Chip Heath & Dan Heath – Switch: How to Change Things When Change Is Hard
- Greg McKeown – Essentialism: The Disciplined Pursuit of Less
- Jack Craven – Aliveness Mindset: Lead and Live with More Passion, Purpose, and Joy

Vulnerability, Trust, and Relationships
- Brené Brown – Dare to Lead; Atlas of the Heart
- Mo Fathelbab – Forum: The Secret Advantage of Successful Leaders
- Ben Sands – Sands Leadership High Growth Leadership Newsletter
- Robert Waldinger & Marc Schulz – The Good Life

Popular Voices and Podcasts
- Robert Glazer – Friday Forward newsletter (robertglazer.com/friday-forward)
- Mel Robbins – Let Them
- Laurie Santos – The Happiness Lab (podcast)

REFERENCES

Abbey, E. (1977). *The journey home: Some words in defense of the American West.* Dutton.

Bartels, M. (2015). Genetics of well-being and its components satisfaction with life, happiness, and quality of life: A review and meta-analysis of heritability studies. *Behavior Genetics, 45*(2), 137–156.

Bartels, M. (2015). Genetics of well-being and its components satisfaction with life, happiness, and depressive symptoms. *Twin Research and Human Genetics, 18*(6), 748–756.

Berg, J. M., Wrzesniewski, A., & Dutton, J. E. (2010). Perceiving and responding to challenges in job crafting at different ranks: When proactivity requires adaptivity. *Journal of Organizational Behavior, 31*(2–3), 158–186.

Brickman, P., & Campbell, D. T. (1971). Hedonic relativism and planning the good society. In M. H. Appley (Ed.), *Adaptation-level theory: A symposium* (pp. 287–305). Academic Press.

Brickman, P., Coates, D., & Janoff-Bulman, R. (1978). Lottery winners and accident victims: Is happiness relative? *Journal of Personality and Social Psychology, 36*(8), 917–927.

Bridges, W. (2004). *Transitions: Making Sense of Life's Changes* (2nd ed.). Da Capo Lifelong Books.

Brooks, A. C. (2022). *From strength to strength: Finding success, happiness, and deep purpose in the second half of life.* Portfolio.

Brooks, D. (2019). *The second mountain: The quest for a moral life.* Random House.

Carstensen, L. L. (2006). The influence of a sense of time on human development. *Science, 312*(5782), 1913–1915.

Charles, S. T., & Carstensen, L. L. (2010). Social and emotional aging. *Annual Review of Psychology, 61*, 383–409.

Clear, J. (2018). *Atomic habits: An easy & proven way to build good habits & break bad ones.* Avery.

Covey, S. R. (1989). *The 7 habits of highly effective people: Powerful lessons in personal change.* Free Press.

C.A.S.T.
Curiosity - Aim - Send It - Tend It & Track

Cowan, N. (2001). The magical number 4 in short-term memory: A reconsideration of mental storage capacity. *Behavioral and Brain Sciences, 24*(1), 87–114.

Craven, J. (2023). *Aliveness mindset: Lead and live with more passion, purpose, and joy.* Forefront Books.

Crowley, C., & Lodge, H. S. (2019). *Younger Next Year: A Guide to Living Like 50 Until You're 80 and Beyond.* Workman Publishing.

Csikszentmihalyi, M. (1990). *Flow: The psychology of optimal experience.* Harper & Row.

David, S. (2016). *Emotional agility: Get unstuck, embrace change, and thrive in work and life.* Avery.

Deci, E. L., & Ryan, R. M. (2000). The "what" and "why" of goal pursuits: Human needs and the self-determination of behavior. *Psychological Inquiry, 11*(4), 227–268.

Dethmer, J., Chapman, D., & Klemp, K. W. (2014). *The 15 Commitments of Conscious Leadership: A New Paradigm for Sustainable Success.* The Conscious Leadership Group.

Diener, E. (1984). Subjective well-being. *Psychological Bulletin, 95*(3), 542–575.

Diener, E., & Biswas-Diener, R. (2002). Will money increase subjective well-being? *Social Indicators Research, 57*(2), 119–169.

Diener, E., Emmons, R. A., Larsen, R. J., & Griffin, S. (1985). The Satisfaction With Life Scale. *Journal of Personality Assessment, 49*(1), 71–75.

Diener, E., Suh, E. M., Lucas, R. E., & Smith, H. L. (1999). Subjective well-being: Three decades of progress. *Psychological Bulletin, 125*(2), 276–302.

Diener, E., Suh, E., Oishi, S., & Lucas, R. E. (2010). Subjective well-being: The science of happiness and life satisfaction. In S. J. Lopez & C. R. Snyder (Eds.), *The Oxford handbook of positive psychology* (2nd ed., pp. 63–73). Oxford University Press.

Diener, E., Wirtz, D., Tov, W., et al. (2010). New well-being measures: Short scales to assess flourishing and positive and negative feelings. *Social Indicators Research, 97*(2), 143–156.

Dunn, E. W., Gilbert, D. T., & Wilson, T. D. (2011). If money doesn't make you happy, then you probably aren't spending it right. *Journal of Consumer Psychology, 21*(2), 115–125.

Dunn, E. W., & Norton, M. I. (2013). *Happy money: The science of happier spending.* Simon & Schuster.

C.A.S.T.
Curiosity - Aim - Send It - Tend It & Track

Edmondson, A. C. (2019). *The fearless organization: Creating psychological safety in the workplace for learning, innovation, and growth.* Wiley.

Fogg, B. J. (2020). *Tiny Habits: The Small Changes That Change Everything.* Houghton Mifflin Harcourt.

Fredrickson, B. L. (2001). The role of positive emotions in positive psychology: The broaden-and-build theory of positive emotions. *American Psychologist, 56*(3), 218–226.

Frederick, S., & Loewenstein, G. (1999). Hedonic adaptation. In D. Kahneman, E. Diener, & N. Schwarz (Eds.), *Well-being: The foundations of hedonic psychology* (pp. 302–329). Russell Sage Foundation.

George, B. (2007). *True north: Discover your authentic leadership.* Jossey-Bass.

Glazer, R. (2025). *The compass within: How to discover your core values and use them to guide your life.* Matt Holt Books.

Gottman, J. M. (1994). *What predicts divorce? The relationship between marital processes and marital outcomes.* Lawrence Erlbaum Associates.

Grant, A. M. (2014). *Give and take: Why helping others drives our success.* Penguin.

Harkin, B., Webb, T. L., Chang, B. P., Prestwich, A., Conner, M., Kellar, I., Benn, Y., & Sheeran, P. (2016). Does monitoring goal progress promote goal attainment? A meta-analysis of the experimental evidence. *Psychological Bulletin, 142*(2), 198–229.

Hackman, J. R., & Oldham, G. R. (1976). Motivation through the design of work: Test of a theory. *Organizational Behavior and Human Performance, 16*(2), 250–279.

Haidt, J. (2006). *The happiness hypothesis: Finding modern truth in ancient wisdom.* Basic Books.

Harris, R. (2009). *ACT made simple: An easy-to-read primer on acceptance and commitment therapy.* New Harbinger.

Harris, R. (2009). *The happiness trap: How to stop struggling and start living.* Trumpeter.

Hayes, S. C., Strosahl, K. D., & Wilson, K. G. (2011). *Acceptance and commitment therapy: The process and practice of mindful change* (2nd ed.). Guilford Press.

Henrich, J., Heine, S. J., & Norenzayan, A. (2010). The weirdest people in the world? *Behavioral and Brain Sciences, 33*(2–3), 61–83.

Henrich, J., Heine, S. J., & Norenzayan, A. (2010). Most people are not WEIRD. *Nature, 466*(7302), 29.

Holt-Lunstad, J., Smith, T. B., Baker, M., Harris, T., & Stephenson, D. (2015). Loneliness and social isolation as risk factors for mortality: A meta-analytic review. *Perspectives on Psychological Science, 10*(2), 227–237.

Holt-Lunstad, J., Smith, T. B., & Layton, J. B. (2010). Social relationships and mortality risk: A meta-analytic review. *PLOS Medicine, 7*(7), e1000316.

House, J. S., Landis, K. R., & Umberson, D. (1988). Social relationships and health. *Science, 241*(4865), 540–545.

Huberman, A. (Host). (2021–present). *Huberman Lab* [Audio podcast]. Scicomm Media.

Kahneman, D. (2011). *Thinking, fast and slow.* Farrar, Straus and Giroux.

Kahneman, D., & Deaton, A. (2010). High income improves evaluation of life but not emotional well-being. *Proceedings of the National Academy of Sciences, 107*(38), 16489–16493.

Kets de Vries, M. F. R. (2005). Leadership group coaching in action: The Zen of creating high performance teams. *Academy of Management Executive, 19*(2), 61–76.

Keyes, C. L. M. (2007). Promoting and protecting mental health as flourishing: A complementary strategy for improving national mental health. *American Psychologist, 62*(2), 95–108.

Killingsworth, M. A. (2021). Experienced well-being rises with income, even above $75,000 per year. *Proceedings of the National Academy of Sciences, 118*(4), e2016976118.

Lencioni, P. (2002). *The five dysfunctions of a team: A leadership fable.* Jossey-Bass.

Levinson, D. J. (1978). *The Seasons of a Man's Life.* Knopf.

Li, Q. (2018). *Forest bathing: How trees can help you find health and happiness.* Penguin.

Lucas, R. E. (2007). Adaptation and the set-point model of subjective well-being: Does happiness change after major life events? *Current Directions in Psychological Science, 16*(2), 75–79.

Lucas, R. E. (2007). Long-term disability is associated with lasting changes in subjective well-being: Evidence from two nationally representative longitudinal studies. *Journal of Personality and Social Psychology, 92*(4), 717–730.

Lucas, R. E., Clark, A. E., Georgellis, Y., & Diener, E. (2003). Reexamining adaptation and the set point model of happiness: Reactions to changes in marital status. *Journal of Personality and Social Psychology, 84*(3), 527–539.

Lucas, R. E., Clark, A. E., Georgellis, Y., & Diener, E. (2004). Unemployment alters the set point for life satisfaction. *Psychological Science, 15*(1), 8–13.

Lykken, D., & Tellegen, A. (1996). Happiness is a stochastic phenomenon. *Psychological Science, 7*(3), 186–189.

Lyubomirsky, S. (2007). *The how of happiness: A scientific approach to getting the life you want.* Penguin.

Lyubomirsky, S., & Lepper, H. S. (1999). A measure of subjective happiness: Preliminary reliability and construct validation. *Social Indicators Research, 46*(2), 137–155.

Lyubomirsky, S., Sheldon, K. M., & Schkade, D. (2005). Pursuing happiness: The architecture of sustainable change. *Review of General Psychology, 9*(2), 111–131.

Maslach, C., & Leiter, M. P. (2016). Understanding the burnout experience: Recent research and its implications for psychiatry. *World Psychiatry, 15*(2), 103–111.

Maslach, C., & Leiter, M. P. (2016). *Burnout: A brief history and how to prevent it.* Harvard Business Review Press.

Maslow, A. H. (1964). *Religions, values, and peak experiences.* Ohio State University Press.

McCrae, R. R., & Costa, P. T., Jr. (1999). A five-factor theory of personality. In L. A. Pervin & O. P. John (Eds.), *Handbook of personality: Theory and research* (2nd ed., pp. 139–153). Guilford Press.

McKeown, G. (2014). *Essentialism: The disciplined pursuit of less.* Crown Business.

Michie, S., Abraham, C., Whittington, C., McAteer, J., & Gupta, S. (2009). Effective techniques in healthy eating and physical activity interventions: A meta-regression. *Health Psychology, 28*(6), 690–701.

Miller, G. A. (1956). The magical number seven, plus or minus two: Some limits on our capacity for processing information. *Psychological Review, 63*(2), 81–97.

Nietzsche, F. (1990). *Twilight of the idols* (R. J. Hollingdale, Trans.). Penguin Books. (Original work published 1889)

Oishi, S., Choi, H., Koo, M., Galinha, I., Ishii, K., Komiya, A., ... & Besser, L. L. (2020). Happiness, meaning, and psychological richness. *Affective Science, 1*(2), 107–115.

Oishi, S., & Westgate, E. C. (2021). A psychologically rich life: Beyond happiness and meaning. *Psychological Review, 128*(4), 790–803.

Patterson, K., Grenny, J., McMillan, R., & Switzler, A. (2012). *Crucial conversations: Tools for talking when stakes are high* (2nd ed.). McGraw-Hill.

Ratey, J. J. (2008). *Spark: The revolutionary new science of exercise and the brain.* Little, Brown.

Riso, D. R., & Hudson, R. (1999). *The wisdom of the Enneagram: The complete guide to psychological and spiritual growth for the nine personality types.* Bantam Books.

Robbins, M. (2024). *Let them: A life-changing tool that millions of people can't stop talking about.* Hay House.

Roberts, B. W., Walton, K. E., & Viechtbauer, W. (2006). Patterns of mean-level change in personality traits across the life course: A meta-analysis of longitudinal studies. *Psychological Bulletin, 132*(1), 1–25.

Ryan, R. M., & Deci, E. L. (2001). On happiness and human potentials: A review of research on hedonic and eudaimonic well-being. *Annual Review of Psychology, 52*, 141–166.

Seligman, M. E. P. (2002). *Authentic happiness: Using the new positive psychology to realize your potential for lasting fulfillment.* Free Press.

Seligman, M. E. P. (2011). *Flourish: A visionary new understanding of happiness and well-being.* Free Press.

Seligman, M. E. P., Steen, T. A., Park, N., & Peterson, C. (2005). Positive psychology progress: Empirical validation of interventions. *American Psychologist, 60*(5), 410–421.

Seligman, M. E. P., & Csikszentmihalyi, M. (2000). Positive psychology: An introduction. *American Psychologist, 55*(1), 5–14.

Sin, N. L., & Lyubomirsky, S. (2009). Enhancing well-being and alleviating depressive symptoms with positive psychology interventions: A practice-friendly meta-analysis. *Journal of Clinical Psychology, 65*(5), 467–487.

Sweller, J. (1988). Cognitive load during problem solving: Effects on learning. *Cognitive Science, 12*(2), 257–285.

Van Boven, L., & Gilovich, T. (2003). To do or to have? That is the question. *Journal of Personality and Social Psychology, 85*(6), 1193–1202.

Vanderkam, L. (2010). *168 hours: You have more time than you think.* Portfolio.

Waldinger, R. J., & Schulz, M. S. (2023). *The good life: Lessons from the world's longest scientific study of happiness.* Simon & Schuster.

C.A.S.T.
Curiosity - Aim - Send It - Tend It & Track

Walker, M. (2017). *Why we sleep: Unlocking the power of sleep and dreams.* Scribner.

Wang, M., & Shi, J. (2014). Psychological research on retirement. *Annual Review of Psychology, 65*, 209–233.

Watson, D., Clark, L. A., & Tellegen, A. (1988). Development and validation of brief measures of positive and negative affect: The PANAS scales. *Journal of Personality and Social Psychology, 54*(6), 1063–1070.

Wickman, G. (2011). *Traction: Get a grip on your business.* BenBella Books.

Wrzesniewski, A., & Dutton, J. E. (2001). Crafting a job: Revisioning employees as active crafters of their work. *Academy of Management Review, 26*(2), 179–201.

ACKNOWLEDGEMENTS

Family and Close Friends - This book would not exist without the steady love, patience, and encouragement of my family and closest friends. Whatever I've learned about a fulfilling life has come as much from relationships as from reflection.

Mom and Dad, you've always been my biggest fans. I love you dearly. I'm also grateful to parents and in-laws who welcomed me as their son: Anne, Gloria, Maggie, Robert, and Walt. To my sister June and her family, thank you for your partnership in caring for our parents as they enter new seasons of life.

To my wife, Rebecca: thank you for being the best life partner I could have hoped for. Your optimism and free spirit are the perfect offset to my tendencies to control and protect. Your support has been the quiet current underneath everything in these pages. This book is better because of your care, honesty, and belief in me.

To my two incredible sons, Cove and Drake: you are the hope and joy in my life and a constant reminder of what truly matters. Many of the "casts" in this book are about trying to become a father you can be proud of.

To my close friends from college—Andy Bressler, Brent Knight, Jeff Hoffman, and Steven Tepper—thank you for a friendship that has lasted across many seasons. You were there when I was an unfocused student, a scattered entrepreneur, an overextended workaholic, and a less available friend as fatherhood took hold. Your loyalty and perspective reminded me that who is in our boat matters as much as where we think we're going.

C.A.S.T.
Curiosity - Aim - Send It - Tend It & Track

Readers, Mentors, and Colleagues Who Shaped This Book - I am deeply grateful to the mentors, friends, clients, and colleagues who read early drafts and offered candid feedback. Your comments helped refine the stories, sharpen the concepts, and ground the book more firmly in the complexity of leadership. You helped me move from rough casts to well-placed ones. In alphabetical order, thank you: Amy Lenert, Arnold Strebe, Ben Sands, Beth Ritter, Eric Robertson, Garrett Berger, Jack Craven, Josh Gentine, Kurt Laufer, Mo Fathelbab, Paula Alexander, and Tom Kiernan.

My YPO Forum peers - Thank you for being thoughtful accountability partners and creating space for honesty and vulnerability: Austin Brockenbrough IV, Clifton Harrell, David Thornhill, Ed Walker, Rich Crawford, Rick Evans, and Tobias Dengel.

Leaders Who Took a Risk on Me - I also want to acknowledge leaders, bosses, managers, recruiters, and sponsors who, over the years, took a risk by hiring, promoting, managing, or referring me to new opportunities. Each of you gave me a chance to lead, to learn, and sometimes to fail and recover. I benefited from your coaching, your patience, and your honest critique. I tried to honor those experiences by translating what I learned into something that might be useful for others. Insights in these pages are built on what I gained working alongside you and under your leadership. In alphabetical order, thank you: Amy Collins, Bill Crutchfield, Bill Knees, Bob Irvin, Brad Irwin, Brian Schulz, Cameron Hardesty, Caryl Rusbult, Carrie Dunne, Claire Patrick, David Gardner, Frank Qiu, Greg Creed, Helayna Minsk, Jim Baker, Jim Geikie, John Replogle, Karen Li, Kim Kapoor, Kim Milligan, Lauren Dunne, Len Johnson, Lesya Lysyj, Michael Judlowe, Michael

Sands, Peter Ryan, Peter Waxman, Rick Routheir, Rick Souder, Rob Olsson, Robert Krist, Sandy Ellis, Ted Wesson, and Ting Xu.

Team Members, Clients and Co-Travelers - I am deeply grateful to the team members who worked alongside me over the years—sometimes under my leadership, sometimes as peers, and often teaching me more than I taught them. To those who supported me even when I stumbled, who challenged my thinking, and who stayed committed to the work—thank you. You shaped how I think about leadership, accountability, and what it means to show up for others. I'm equally grateful to the clients who trusted me with their stories, challenges, and hopes. It's been a privilege to walk alongside you, to offer support, and to witness the weight you carry and your impact. Your willingness to think out loud with me, to be honest about what was difficult, and to introduce me to your colleagues expanded my world far beyond what I would have achieved on my own. The list of team members and clients who shaped this book is too long to name individually, but countless conversations with you informed the questions, examples, and practices in these pages. This book is richer because so many of you were willing to keep casting toward a life of greater impact and fulfillment—and invited me to join you.

A Note on the Use of AI - In the spirit of using the best tools available, I used artificial intelligence as a behind-the-scenes assistant. AI helped with editing, flow, and exploring alternative ways to express key ideas. The stories, experiences, and judgments are my own; the technology simply sharpened their expression.

C.A.S.T.
Curiosity - Aim - Send It - Tend It & Track

ABOUT THE AUTHOR

On a great day, you can plot the arc of John Haydock's life from a riverbank. Fly fishing started as a pastime and became something else: a way to slow down, look beneath the surface, and notice what really matters—a thread that runs through his work and this book. Over the years, he organized his life around a handful of values: Responsibility, Independence, Sustainability, Health, and Empathy. Those values were shaped by both the responsibilities of leadership—bootstrapping a struggling business in college, leading multi-brand portfolios through growth, serving on nonprofit boards, and raising a family—and by the sustaining forces outside of work: enduring friendships, volunteer service to causes he cares about, and time outdoors that restores clarity and perspective. John studied psychology as an undergraduate, sparking a curiosity about how people think, feel, and relate. That background, followed by an MBA, set him up for a career at the intersection of human behavior and business realities. For over thirty years, he built brands and teams at organizations including Unilever, Cadbury Schweppes, Crutchfield, and Plow & Hearth, among others. He served in roles from SVP, President, COO, and board member. He led businesses from startups to portfolios with over $1 billion in sales. Since 2011, he's been part of a peer forum with Young Presidents' Organization (YPO) members, focused on leadership and growth. He held leadership positions on nonprofit boards including American Rivers, where he served as Vice Chair and Board Chair. Today, through Sight Casting Consulting, John serves as coach, advisor, and fractional leader to founders, CEOs, and leadership teams. He lives in Charlottesville, Virginia, with his wife and two sons. When he isn't coaching or consulting, he is likely on a river with a fly rod—working out the questions of happiness, fulfillment, and sustainable effort this book explores.

C.A.S.T.
Curiosity - Aim - Send It - Tend It & Track

www.ingramcontent.com/pod-product-compliance
Lightning Source LLC
Chambersburg PA
CBHW070623030426
42337CB00020B/3894